Money, and
the Law of
Attraction

Other Hay House Titles by Esther and Jerry Hicks

(The Teachings of Abraham®)

Books, Calendar, and Card Decks

The Law of Attraction (also available in Spanish)
The Amazing Power of Deliberate Intent (also available in Spanish)
Ask and It Is Given (also available in Spanish)
Ask and It Is Given Cards
Ask and It Is Given Perpetual Flip Calendar
The Astonishing Power of Emotions (available in Spanish in 2009)
The Law of Attraction Cards
Manifest Your Desires
Relationships, and the Law of Attraction (book; 5-CD set—both available June 2009)
Sara, Book 1: Sara Learns the Secret about the <u>Law of Attraction</u>
Sara, Book 2: Solomon's Fine Featherless Friends
Sara, Book 3: A Talking Owl Is Worth a Thousand Words!
Spirituality, and the Law of Attraction (book; 5-CD set—both available September 2010)
The Teachings of Abraham Well-Being Cards

Additional CD Programs

The Teachings of Abraham Master Course Audio (11-CD set)
The Law of Attraction (4-CD set)
The Law of Attraction in Action (2-DVD set)
The Amazing Power of Deliberate Intent (Parts I and II: two 4-CD sets)
Ask and It Is Given (Parts I and II: two 4-CD sets)
The Astonishing Power of Emotions (8-CD set)
Sara, Books 1, 2, 3 (unabridged audio books; 3-CD sets)

DVD Programs

The Law of Attraction in Action, Episodes I, II, III, IV, V, VI (2-DVD sets)
The Teachings of Abraham Master Course Video (5-DVD set)
The Secret Behind "The Secret"? (Abraham) (2-DVD set)

⁓⁌ ▦ ⁍⁓

Please visit Hay House USA: **www.hayhouse.com**®
Hay House Australia: **www.hayhouse.com.au**
Hay House UK: **www.hayhouse.co.uk**
Hay House South Africa: **www.hayhouse.co.za**
Hay House India: **www.hayhouse.co.in**

Money, and the Law of Attraction

Learning to Attract Wealth, Health, and Happiness

ESTHER AND JERRY HICKS

(The Teachings of Abraham®)

HAY HOUSE, INC.

Carlsbad, California • New York City
London • Sydney • Johannesburg
Vancouver • Hong Kong • New Delhi

Published and distributed in the United States by: Hay House, Inc.: www.hayhouse.
com • *Published and distributed in Australia by:* Hay House Australia Pty. Ltd.:
www.hayhouse.com.au • *Published and distributed in the United Kingdom by:* Hay
House UK, Ltd.: www.hayhouse.co.uk • *Published and distributed in the Republic
of South Africa by:* Hay House SA (Pty), Ltd.: www.hayhouse.co.za • *Distributed
in Canada by:* Raincoast: www.raincoast.com • *Published in India by:* Hay House
Publishers India: www.hayhouse.co.in

Editorial supervision: Jill Kramer • *Design:* Tricia Breidenthal
Indexer: Richard Comfort: **www.comfortindexing.com**

Library of Congress Cataloging-in-Publication Data

Hicks, Esther.
  Money, and the law of attraction : learning to attract wealth, health, and
happiness / Esther and Jerry Hicks (The Teachings of Abraham).
     p. cm.
  Includes index.
  ISBN-13: 978-1-4019-1881-1 (tradepaper)
  ISBN-13: 978-1-4019-1874-3 (hardcover) 1. Success. 2. New Thought. 3.
Money. 4. Health. 5. Well-being. I. Hicks, Jerry. II. Title.
  BF637.S8H475 2008
  133.9'3--dc22
                                    2008003081

Hardcover ISBN: 978-1-4019-1874-3
Tradepaper ISBN: 978-1-4019-1881-1

11 10 09 08 4 3 2 1
1st edition, August 2008

Printed in the United States of America

—∘⊰[☒]⊱∘—

*We have had the pleasure of meeting with some of the
most influential people of our time, and we know of no
one person who is more of a fountainhead for the outpouring
of positive upliftment than Louise Hay (Lulu), the founder of
Hay House—for guided by Lulu's vision, Hay House, Inc.,
has now become the world's largest disseminator
of spiritual and self-improvement materials.*

*And so, to Louise Hay—and to each person she has attracted to her
vision—we lovingly and with much appreciation dedicate this book.*

—∘⊰[☒]⊱∘—

Contents

PART II: Attracting Money and Manifesting Abundance

PART V: Careers, as Profitable Sources of Pleasure

Transcript of Abraham Live: A <u>Law of Attraction</u> Workshop

Preface

by Jerry Hicks

What do you believe attracted you to this book? Why do you suppose you're reading these words? Which part of the title got your attention? Was it *Money? Health? Happiness? Learning to Attract?* Or was it the *Law of Attraction* perhaps?

Whatever the obvious reason may have been for your attention to this book, the information contained here has come to you in answer to something for which you have been somehow asking.

What is this book about? It teaches that life is supposed to feel good and that our overall Well-Being is what is natural. It teaches that no matter how good your life is now, it can always get better, and that the choice and the power to improve your life experience is within your personal control. And it offers practical philosophical tools that—when put into consistent use—will enable you to allow yourself to experience more of the wealth, health, and happiness that is your natural birthright. (And I know, because it keeps happening to me. As I move forward from each desire-clarifying experience of contrast to a new desire and then to a new manifestation—my life overall gets better and better.)

Life is good! It is New Year's Day of 2008, and I'm beginning this Preface while seated at the dining-room table of our new Del Mar, California, "haven."

From the time Esther and I were married (1980), we've been making it a point to visit this "Garden of Eden" area as often as has been practical. And now, after all those years as appreciative San Diego visitors, we will be actually living here as appreciative part-time residents.

And what's not to appreciate? There was our friend who led us to find the property. (We told him we were looking for a piece of property near Del Mar where we could park our 45-foot tour bus.) There were the landscape architects, engineers, designers, carpenters, electricians, plumbers, tile roofers, and copper gutterers. There were those talented, skilled tradespeople: tile layers; stuccoers; painters; and fence, gate, and ironworks creators. There were floor installers and custom-lift, slide-doors, arched-wooden-windows-and-doors, and stained-glass-window folks. There were the "high end" high-tech people who installed the Lutron master-controlled lighting system, the audio/video/computer networking system, the new Trane multiple-zone master-controlled (silent) air-conditioning system, and the Snaidero/Miele/Bosch/Viking kitchen and laundry equipment. There were those who placed our new furniture, and placed it again, and again—as we discovered what felt best. There were those teams of hardworking diggers, trenchers, haulers, cement pourers, stoneworkers, and transplanters of full-grown trees. . . . And then there were the thousands of people who had a hand in—and also earned money from—the invention, creation, and distribution of the thousands of products involved. . . . Well, that's a lot to appreciate.

And that was just the tip of the iceberg of what's to appreciate. There was the discovery of a new "favorite" restaurant—and owners and staff—only a couple of minutes away, and then there were those incredibly delightful eclectic, positive neighbors who welcomed us here in a style that we have never previously experienced.

There's more, too. There's the breathtaking view to the south into the primitive Torrey Pines State Reserve, across the Carmel Valley Creek and waterbird sanctuary and the lagoon, and down into the crashing, foaming waves of the Pacific Ocean as it untiringly washes up onto Torrey Pines Beach. Yes. Life is good!

(Esther and I just finished a brief walk on the beach, and we're now settling down for the evening to put some finishing touches on Abraham's newest book—*Money, and the Law of Attraction: Learning to Attract Wealth, Health, and Happiness.*)

It was over 40 years ago, while performing a series of concerts in colleges across the nation, that I "accidentally" noticed a book lying on a coffee table in a motel in a small town in Montana. That book, Napoleon Hill's *Think and Grow Rich,* changed my beliefs about money so dramatically that my use of its principles attracted financial success to me in a way I hadn't previously imagined.

Thinking or growing rich hadn't been something I had much interest in. But shortly before discovering that book, I *had* decided that I wanted to modify the way I earned money—and increase the amount I received. And so, it turned out that my attraction to Hill's book was a direct answer to what I had been "asking" for.

Soon after encountering *Think and Grow Rich* in that Montana motel, I met a man in a motel in Minnesota who offered me a business opportunity that was so compatible with Hill's teachings that for nine joyous years I focused my attention on building that business. During those nine years, the business grew into a multimillion-dollar international enterprise. And in that relatively short time, my finances grew from just getting by (which was all I'd previously really wanted) to reaching all of my newly inspired financial goals.

What I learned from Hill's book worked so grandly for me that I began using that work as a "textbook" to share his success principles with my business associates. But, looking back, even though the teachings had worked extremely well for me, I became aware that only a couple of my associates had received the huge financial success that I had wanted all of them to have. And so, I began to search for another level of answers that might be more effective for a broader range of people.

As a result of my personal *Think and Grow Rich* experience, I became convinced that the achievement of success was something that could be *learned*. We didn't have to be born into a family who had already discovered how to make money. We didn't have to get good grades in school or know the right people or live in the right country or be the right size, color, gender, religion, and so on. . . . We simply had to learn a few simple principles and then consistently put them into practice.

However, not everyone gets the same message from the same words—or the same results from the same books. And so, as soon as I began "asking" for more understanding, Richard Bach's enlightening book *Illusions* happened to come into my awareness. And although *Illusions* brought me to one of the most thrilling "Aha!" days of my life and brought some concepts that began to open my mind for the phenomenon that I was about to experience, it contained no additional principles that I could consciously utilize in my business.

The next "accidental" discovery of an ultimately valuable book for me came while I was just killing some time in a Phoenix library. I wasn't "looking for" anything, but I happened to notice a book, high on a shelf, entitled *Seth Speaks*, by Jane Roberts and Robert F. Butts. Seth, "a Non-Physical Entity," had "dictated" through Jane a series of books, and I read them all. And as strange as that form of communication may have seemed to most (Esther was extremely uncomfortable with it at first), I had always tended to judge the trees by their fruits. And so, I looked beyond the "strange" aspects and focused on what to me were the positive, practical parts of the Seth material that I felt I could utilize to help others improve their life experience.

Seth had a different perspective on life than what I had heard previously expressed, and I was particularly interested in two of Seth's terms: "You Create Your Own Reality" and "Your Point of Power Is in the Present." Although as much as I read, I never felt that I truly understood those principles, I somehow knew that there were, within them, answers to my questions. However, Jane was no longer in physical form, so "Seth" was unavailable for any further clarification.

Through a series of fortuitous events—in a manner similar to the Seth-and-Jane experiences—Esther, my wife, began receiving the material that is now known as the *Teachings of Abraham®*. (Should you like to hear one of the original recordings detailing our introduction to Abraham, you can find our free *Introduction to*

Abraham recording as a 70-minute download at our Website: **www. abraham-hicks.com**, or from our office as a free CD.)

In 1985 when this phenomenon began with Esther, I could sense that this would bring the answers to my desire to better understand the *Laws of the Universe* and how we might be able to naturally, deliberately work in harmony with them in order to fulfill our purpose for being in physical form. And so, about 20 years ago, I sat with Esther and a small cassette tape recorder and plied Abraham with hundreds of questions on primarily 20 different subjects, mostly regarding practical spirituality. And then, as other people began hearing about Abraham and wanting to interact with us, we produced those 20 recordings and published them as two special-subjects albums.

Over the course of two decades, millions of people have become aware of the Teachings of Abraham as a result of our many books, tapes, CDs, videos, DVDs, group workshops, and radio and television appearances. Also, other best-selling authors soon began to use Abraham's teachings in their books and radio, television, and workshop appearances . . . and then, about two years ago, an Australian television producer approached us requesting permission to build a TV series around our work with Abraham. She joined us with her film crew on one of our Alaskan cruises, filmed the show, and then went in search of other students of our teachings whom she could incorporate into the (pilot) film—and the rest is (as they say) history.

The producer called her movie *The Secret,* and it featured the basic tenet of the Teachings of Abraham: the *Law of Attraction.* And although it wasn't picked up by the Australian network (Nine) as a series, the documentary went straight to the DVD format and was transcribed into a book . . . and now because of *The Secret,* the concept of the *Law of Attraction* has reached many more millions of people who have been asking for a better-feeling life.

This book has evolved from the transcription of five of our original recordings from over 20 years ago. This is the first time these transcriptions have been available in print. However, they're not word for word because Abraham has now gone through every page of the original transcriptions and modified every part that might be made easier for the reader to understand and to put into immediate practical use.

There's a saying in the teaching world: "Tell them what you're going to tell them. Then tell them. And then tell them what you told them." And so, should you decide to immerse yourself in these teachings, you'll probably notice much repetition as you move forward, because we usually learn best through repetition. You can't continue the same old habitual, limiting thought patterns and get new, unlimited results. But through simple, practiced repetition, you can, over time, comfortably develop new life-enhancing habits.

In the media world there's a saying: "People would rather be entertained than informed." Well, unless you're entertained by learning new ways of looking at life, you'll probably find this book more informative than entertaining. Rather than being like a novel that's read, enjoyed, and then set aside, this—more like a textbook on the principles of achieving and maintaining wealth, health, and happiness—is a book to be read and studied and put into practiced use.

I was led to this information by my desire to help others feel better, especially in the area of financial fulfillment, so I feel especially gratified that this *Money* book is now on its way to those who are asking the questions that it will answer.

This book, *Money, and the Law of Attraction,* is the second of four scheduled *Law of Attraction* books. Two years ago we published *The Law of Attraction: The Basics of the Teachings of Abraham.* Next will be *Relationships, and the Law of Attraction;* and the final book in the series will be *Spirituality, and the Law of Attraction.*

Revisiting this life-changing material in preparation for the publication of this book has been a delightful experience for Esther and me, for we've been reminded again of these basic and simple principles that Abraham discussed with us in the beginning of our interaction.

From the beginning, Esther and I have intended to apply to our lives what Abraham has been teaching. And our resulting joyous growth experience has been remarkable: After two decades of practicing these principles, Esther and I are still in love. (Even though we have just now completed building this new home in

California and are in the process of the construction of a new home on our Texas business complex, we enjoy being with each other so much that we will still spend most of next year traveling in our 45-foot-long Marathon motor coach from workshop to workshop.) We've had no medical examinations (or insurance) for 20 years. We're debt free, and will pay more income taxes this year than the sum of all the money we earned in all of our earning years before Abraham's guidance—and although neither all our money nor all of our good health can *make* us happy, Esther and I are still finding ways to be happy anyway.

And so, it is with extraordinary joy that we can tell you—from our own personal experience: *This works!*

ఆోఆోఆో ჩ჈ ჩ჈ ჩ჈

(**Editor's Note:** Please note that since there aren't always physical English words to perfectly express the Non-Physical thoughts that Esther receives, she sometimes forms new combinations of words, as well as using standard words in new ways—for example, capitalizing them when normally they wouldn't be—in order to express new ways of looking at old ways of looking at life.)

PART I

Pivoting
and the *Book* of
Positive Aspects

Your Story, and the *Law of Attraction*

Each and every component that makes up your life experience is drawn to you by the powerful <u>Law of Attraction</u>'s response to the thoughts you think and the story you tell about your life. Your money and financial assets; your body's state of wellness, clarity, flexibility, size, and shape; your work environment, how you are treated, work satisfaction, and rewards—indeed, the very happiness of your life experience in general— is all happening because of the story that you tell. If you will let your dominant intention be to revise and improve the content of the story you tell every day of your life, it is our absolute promise to you that your life will become that ever-improving story. For by the powerful <u>Law of Attraction,</u> it must be!

Does Life Sometimes Seem to Be Unfair?

You have wanted more success and you have applied yourself well, doing everything that everyone said you should do, but the success you have been seeking has been slow to come. You tried very hard, especially at first, to learn all the right things, to be in the right places, to do the right things, to say the right things . . . but often things did not appear to be improving much at all.

Earlier in your life, when you were first dipping your toe into the idea of achieving success, you found satisfaction in satisfying the expectations of the others who were laying out the rules for success. The teachers, parents, and mentors who surrounded you seemed confident and convincing as they laid out their rules for success:

"Always be on time; always do your best; remember to work hard; always be honest; strive for greatness; go the extra mile; there's no gain without pain; and, most important, never give up. . . ."

But, over time, your finding satisfaction from gaining the approval of those who laid out those rules waned as their principles of success—no matter how hard you tried—did not yield you the promised results. And it was more disheartening still when you stood back to gain some perspective on the whole picture and realized that their principles were not, for the most part, bringing *them* real success either. And then, to make matters even worse, you began meeting others (who clearly were *not* following those rules) who *were* achieving success apart from the formula that you had been so diligent to learn and apply.

And so you found yourself asking: "What's going on here? How can those who are working so hard be receiving so little, while those who seem to be working so little are achieving so much? My expensive education hasn't paid off at all—and yet that multimil-lionaire dropped out of high school. My father worked hard every day of his life—and yet our family had to borrow the money to pay for his funeral. . . . Why doesn't my hard work pay off for me the way it was supposed to? Why do so few really get rich, while most of us struggle to barely get by? What am I missing? What do those financially successful people know that I don't know?"

Is "Doing Your Best" Still Not Enough?

When you are doing everything you can think of, truly trying your best to do what you have been told is supposed to bring you success, and success does not come, it is easy to feel defensive, and eventually even angry at those who are displaying evidence of the success you desire. You even find yourself sometimes condemning their success simply because it is too painful to watch them living the success that continues to elude you. And it is for this reason—in response to this chronic condition in the financial affairs of your culture—that we offer this book.

When you come to the place of openly condemning the financial success that you crave, not only can that financial success never come to you, but you are also forfeiting your God-given rights to your health and happiness as well.

Many actually come to the incorrect conclusion that others in their physical environment have banded together in some sort of conspiracy to keep them from succeeding. For they believe, with all of their heart, that they have done everything possible to achieve success, and the fact that it has not come must surely mean that there are some unfriendly forces at work that are depriving them of what they desire. But we want to assure you that nothing like that is at the heart of the absence of what you desire or of the presence of things you would like to remove from your experience. No one ever has or ever could have prevented your success—or provided it. Your success is all up to you. It is all in your control. And we are writing this book so that now, finally, once and for all time, your success can be in your deliberate and conscious control.

Whatever I Can Desire, I Can Achieve

It is time for you to return to the true nature of your Being and to consciously live the success that the experiencing of your own life has helped you determine that you desire. And so, as you deliberately relax right now, breathing deeply and reading steadily, you will begin to gradually but surely remember how all success comes, for you already inherently understand it, and so you will certainly feel resonance with these absolute truths as you read about them here.

The Eternal *Laws of the Universe* are consistent and reliable and steadily hold, always, the promise of expansion and joy. They are being presented to you here in a powerful rhythm of understanding that will start small within you and then expand with each page you read, until you reawaken into the knowledge of your purpose and your own personal power as you remember how to access the power of the Universe that creates worlds.

If this time-space reality has within it the ability to inspire a desire within you, it is absolute that this time-space reality has the ability to yield you a full and satisfying manifestation of that same desire. It is Law.

To Achieve Success Is My Natural Birthright

Most people naturally assume that if their life is not going the way they want it to go, something outside of themselves must be preventing the improvement, for no one would deliberately hold their own success away. But while pointing the blame at others may feel better than assuming responsibility for unwanted conditions, there is a very big negative repercussion to believing that something outside of you is the reason for your own lack of success: *When you give the credit or the blame to another for your success or lack of it—you are powerless to make any change.*

When you desire success, but—from your perspective—you are not currently experiencing it, at many deep levels of your Being you recognize that something is wrong. And as this strong feeling of personal discord magnifies your awareness that you are not getting what you want, it often sets into motion other counterproductive assumptions that evoke jealousy toward those who *are* having more success; resentment at a myriad of people you would like to blame for your lack of success; or even self-denigration, which is the most painful and counterproductive assumption of all. And we submit that this uncomfortable upheaval is not only normal, but it is the perfect response to your feeling a lack of success.

Your emotional discomfort is a powerful indicator that something is very wrong. You are meant to succeed, and failure *should* feel bad to you. You are meant to be well, and sickness *should not* be accepted. You are supposed to expand, and stagnation *is* intolerable. Life is supposed to go well for you—and when it does not, there *is* something wrong.

But what is wrong is not that an injustice has occurred, or that the gods of good fortune are not focusing on you, or that someone else has received the success that should have been yours. What is wrong is that you are out of harmony with your own Being, with *who-you-really-are,* with what life has caused you to ask for, with what you have expanded to, and with the ever-consistent *Laws of the Universe. What is wrong is not something that is outside of you over which you have no control. What is wrong is within you—and you <u>do</u> have control. And taking control is not difficult to do once you understand the basis of <u>who-you-are</u> and the basics of the <u>Law of Attraction</u> and the value of your personal <u>Emotional Guidance System</u> that you were born with, which is always active, ever present, and easy to understand.*

Money Is Not the Root of Evil or of Happiness

This important subject of *money* and *financial success* is not the "root of all evil" as many have quoted—nor is it the path to happiness. However, because the subject of money touches most of you in one way or another hundreds or even thousands of times in every day, it is a large factor in your vibrational makeup and in your personal point of attraction. So when you are able to successfully control something that affects most of you all day, every day, you will have accomplished something rather significant. In other words, because such a high percentage of your thoughts in any given day reside around the topic of money or financial success, as soon as you are able to *deliberately* guide your thoughts, not only is it certain that your financial success must improve, but the evidence of *that* success will then prepare you for deliberate improvement in *every* aspect of your life experience.

If you are a student of *Deliberate Creation,* if you want to consciously create your own reality, if you desire control of your own life experience, if you want to fulfill your reason for being, then your understanding of these prevalent topics—*money and the <u>Law of Attraction</u>*—will serve you enormously well.

I Am the Attractor of My Every Experience

You are meant to live an expansive, exhilarating, good-feeling experience. It was your plan when you made the decision to become focused in your physical body in this time-space reality. You expected this physical life to be exciting and rewarding. In other words, you knew that the variety and contrast would stimulate you to expanded desires, and you also knew that any and all of those desires could be fully and easily realized by you. You knew, also, that there would be no end to the expansion of new desires.

You came into your body full of excitement about the possibilities that this life experience would inspire, and that desire that you held in the beginning was not muted at all by trepidation or doubt, for you knew your power and you knew that this life experience and all of its contrast would be the fertile ground for wonderful expansion. *Most of all, you knew that you were coming into this life experience with a* Guidance System *to help you remain true to your original intent as well as to your never-ending amended intentions that would be born out of this very life experience. In short, you felt an eagerness for this time-space reality that nearly defies physical description.*

You were not a beginner—even though you were newly beginning in your wee, small physical body—but instead you were a powerful creative genius, newly focusing in a new, Leading Edge environment. You knew that there would be a time of adjustment while redefining a new platform from which you would begin your process of deliberate creating, and you were not the least bit worried about that time of adjustment. In fact, you rather enjoyed the nest into which you were born and those who were there to greet you into your new physical environment. And while you could not yet speak the language of their words—and although you were perceived by those who greeted you as new and unknowing and in need of their guidance—you possessed a stability and a knowing that most of them had long left behind.

You were born knowing that you are a powerful Being, that you are good, that you are the creator of your experience, and that the *Law of Attraction* is the basis of all creation here in your new environment. You remembered then that the *Law of Attraction* (the essence of that which is like unto itself, is drawn) is the basis of the Universe, and you knew it would serve you well. And so it has.

You were still remembering then that you are the creator of your own experience. But even more important, you remembered that you do it through your *thought, not your action.* You were not uncomfortable being a small infant who offered no action or words, for you remembered the Well-Being of the Universe; you remembered your intentions in coming forth into your physical body, and you knew that there would be plenty of time for acclimating to the language and ways of your new environment; and, most of all, you knew that even though you would not be able to translate your vast knowledge from your Non-Physical environment directly into physical words and descriptions, it would not matter, for the most important things to set you on a path of joyful creation were already emphatically in place: You knew that the *Law of Attraction* was consistently present and that your *Guidance System* was immediately active. And, most of all, you knew that by trial, and what some may call "error," you would eventually become completely and consciously reoriented in your new environment.

I Knew of the Consistency of the *Law of Attraction*

The fact that the *Law of Attraction* remains constant and stable throughout the Universe was a big factor in your confidence as you came into your new physical environment, for you knew that the feedback of life would help you to remember and gain your footing. You remembered that the basis of everything is *vibration* and that the *Law of Attraction* responds to those vibrations and, in essence, organizes them, bringing things of like vibrations together while holding those not of like vibrations apart.

And so, you were not concerned about not being able to articulate that knowledge right away or to explain it to those around you who had seemingly forgotten everything they knew about it, because you knew that the consistency of this powerful *Law* would, soon enough, show itself to you through the examples of your own life. You knew then that it would not be difficult to figure out what kinds of vibrations you were offering because the *Law of Attraction* would be bringing to you constant evidence of whatever your vibration was.

In other words, when you feel *overwhelmed,* circumstances and people who could help you get out from under your feeling of overwhelment cannot find you, nor can you find them. Even when you try hard to find them, you cannot. And those people who *do* come do not help you, but, instead, they add to your feeling of overwhelment.

When you feel *mistreated*—fairness cannot find you. Your perception of your mistreatment, and the subsequent vibration that you offer because of your perception, prevents anything that you would consider to be fair from coming to you.

When you are buried in the *disappointment* or *fear* of not having the financial resources that you believe you need, the dollars—or the opportunities that would bring the dollars—continue to elude you . . . not because you are bad or unworthy, but because the *Law of Attraction* matches things that are like, not things that are *un*like.

When you feel *poor*—only things that feel like *poverty* can come to you. When you feel *prosperous*—only things that feel like *prosperity* can come to you. This *Law* is consistent; and if you will pay attention, it will teach you, through life experience, how it works. *When you remember that you get the essence of what you think about—and then you notice what you are getting—you have the keys for Deliberate Creation.*

What Do We Mean by *Vibration?*

When we speak of *vibration,* we are actually calling your attention to the basis of your experience, for everything is actually *vibrationally* based. We could use the word *Energy* interchangeably, and there are many other synonyms in your vocabulary that accurately apply.

Most understand the vibrational characteristics of sound. Sometimes when the deep, rich bass notes of your musical instrumentation are played loudly, you can even *feel* the vibrational nature of sound.

We want you to understand that whenever you "hear" something, you are interpreting vibration into the sound you are hearing. What you hear is *your* interpretation of vibration; what you hear is your *unique* interpretation of vibration. Each of your physical senses of seeing, hearing, tasting, smelling, and touching exist because everything in the Universe is vibrating and your physical senses are reading the vibrations and giving you sensory perception of the vibrations.

So as you come to understand that you live in a pulsating, vibrating Universe of advanced harmonics, and that at the very core of your Being you are vibrating at what could only be described as perfection in vibrational balance and harmony, then you begin to understand *vibration* in the way we are projecting it.

Everything that exists, in your air, in your dirt, in your water, and in your bodies, is vibration in motion—and all of it is managed by the powerful Law of Attraction.

You could not sort it out if you wanted to. And there is no need for you to sort it out, because the *Law of Attraction* is doing the sorting, continually bringing things of like vibrations together while things of different vibrational natures are being repelled.

Your emotions, which really are the most powerful and important of your six physical vibrational interpreters, give you constant feedback about the harmonics of your current thoughts (vibrations) as they compare with the harmonics of your core vibrational state.

The Non-Physical world is vibration.

The physical world that you know is vibration.

There is nothing that exists outside of this vibrational nature.

There is nothing that is not managed by the *Law of Attraction*.

Your understanding of vibration will help you to consciously bridge both worlds.

You do not have to understand your complex optic nerve or your primary visual cortex in order to see. You do not have to understand electricity to be able to turn on the light, and you do not have to understand vibrations in order to feel the difference between harmony or discord.

As you learn to accept your vibrational nature, and begin to consciously utilize your emotional vibrational indicators, you will gain conscious control of your personal creations and of the outcomes of your life experience.

Whenever I Feel Abundant, Abundance Finds Me

When you make the conscious correlation between what you have been feeling and what is actualizing in your life experience, now you are empowered to make changes. If you are not making that correlation, and so continue to offer thoughts of lack about things you want, the things you want will continue to elude you.

People, often, in this misunderstanding begin to assign power to things outside of themselves in order to explain why they are not thriving in the way they would like: "I'm not thriving because I was born into the wrong environment. I'm not thriving because my parents didn't thrive, so they couldn't teach me how to do it. I'm not thriving because those people over there are thriving, and they're taking the resources that should have been mine. I'm not thriving because I was cheated, because I'm not worthy, because I didn't live the right way in a past life, because my government ignores my rights, because my husband doesn't do his part . . . because, because, because."

And we want to remind you, your "not thriving" is only because you are offering a vibration that is different from the vibration of thriving. *You cannot feel poor (and vibrate poor) and thrive. Abundance cannot find you unless you offer a vibration of abundance.*

Many ask, "But if I'm not thriving, then how in the world can I offer a vibration of thriving? Don't I have to thrive before I can offer the vibration of thriving?" We agree that it is certainly easy to maintain a condition of thriving when it is already in your experience, because then all you have to do is notice the good that is coming and your observation of it will keep it coming. But if you are standing in the absence of something you want, you must find a way to feel the essence of it—even before it comes—or it cannot come.

You cannot let your vibrational offering come only in response to *what-is* and then ever change *what-is*. You must find a way of *feeling* the excitement or satisfaction of your currently unrealized dreams before those dreams can become your reality. Find a way to deliberately imagine a scenario for the purpose of offering a vibration and for the purpose of the *Law of Attraction* matching your vibration with a real-life manifestation. . . . *When you ask for the manifestation prior to the vibration, you ask the impossible. When you are willing to offer the vibration before the manifestation—all things are possible. It is Law.*

Rather Than by Default, Live Life Deliberately

We are giving this book to you to remind you of things you already know at some level, so as to reactivate that vibrational knowledge within you. It is not possible for you to read these words, which represent the knowledge that you hold from your Broader Perspective, without a recognition of this knowledge beginning to surface from within.

This really is the time of awakening—the time of remembering your personal power and your reason for being. So take a deep breath, make an effort to get comfortable, and slowly read the contents of this book to restore yourself to your original vibrational essence. . . .

So here you are, in a wonderful state of being: no longer an infant under the control of others, somewhat acclimated into your physical environment, and now—by reading this book—returning to the recognition of the full power of your Being . . . no longer buffeted around by the *Law of Attraction* like a small cork on a raging sea, but finally remembering and gaining control of your own destiny, finally and *deliberately* guiding your life within the powerful *Law of Attraction* rather than responding in an attitude of default and just taking life as it comes. *In order to do that, you have to tell a different story. You have to begin to tell the story of your life as you now want it to be and discontinue the tales of how it has been or of how it is.*

Tell the Story You Want to Experience

To live deliberately, you have to think deliberately; and in order to do that, you must have a reference point in order to determine the correct direction of your thought. Right now, just as at the time of your birth, the two necessary factors are in place. The *Law of Attraction* (the most powerful and consistent *Law* in the Universe) abounds. And your *Guidance System* is within you, all queued up and ready to give you directional feedback. *You have only one seemingly small but potentially life-changing thing to do:* <u>*You have to begin*</u> <u>*telling your story in a new way. You have to tell it as you want it to be.*</u>

As you tell the story of your life (and you do it nearly all day, every day with your words, your thoughts, and your actions), you have to feel good while you tell it. *In every moment, about every subject, you can focus positively or negatively, for in every particle of the Universe—in every moment in time and beyond—there is that which is wanted and the lack of what is wanted pulsing there for you to choose between.* And as these constant choices reveal themselves to you, you have the option of focusing upon what you want or the lack of it regarding every subject, because every subject is really two subjects: what you want or the absence of what you want. You can tell, by the way you feel, which choice you are currently focused upon—and you can change your choice constantly.

Every Subject Is Really Two Subjects

The following are some examples to help you see how every subject is really two subjects:

Abundance/Poverty (absence of abundance)
Health/Illness (absence of health)
Happiness/Sadness (absence of happiness)
Clarity/Confusion (absence of clarity)
Energetic/Tired (absence of Energy)
Knowledge/Doubt (absence of knowledge)
Interested/Bored (absence of interest)

I can do that/I can't do that
I want to buy that/I can't afford that
I want to feel good/I don't feel good
I want more money/I don't have enough money
I want more money/I don't know how to get more money
I want more money/That person is getting more money than
    his/her share
I want to be slender/I am fat
I want a new car/My car is old
I want a lover/I don't have a lover

As you read this list, it is undoubtedly obvious to you which we consider to be the better choice in each example, but there is a simple and important thing that you may be forgetting. There is a tendency as you read a list such as this to feel a need to state the factual truth about the subject ("tell it like it is") rather than make the statement of what you desire. That tendency alone is responsible for more miscreating and more personal disallowing of wanted things than all other things put together, and so, the examples and exercises offered in this book are given to help you orient yourself toward what is *wanted,* not to explain what already *is. You have to begin telling a different story if you want the <u>Law of Attraction</u> to bring you different things.*

What Is the Story I'm Now Telling?

A very effective way to begin to tell that new story is to listen to the things that you are now saying throughout your day, and when you catch yourself in the middle of a statement that is contrary to what you want, stop and say, "Well, I clearly know what it is that I *don't* want. What is it that I *do* want?" Then deliberately and emphatically make your statement of desire.

I hate this ugly, old, unreliable car.
I want a pretty, new, reliable car.

I'm fat.
I want to be slender.

My employer doesn't appreciate me.
I want to be appreciated by my employer.

Many would protest, claiming that a simple rewording of a sentence will not make a shiny new car appear in your driveway, or change your fat body to one that is slender, or cause your employer to suddenly change her personality and begin to treat you differently—but they would be wrong. When you deliberately focus upon any desired subject, often proclaiming it to be as you *want* it to be, in time you experience an actual shift in the way you feel about the subject, which indicates a vibrational shift.

When your vibration shifts, your point of attraction shifts, and, by the powerful Law of Attraction, your manifestational evidence or indicator must shift, also. You cannot talk consistently of the things you do want to experience in your life without the Universe delivering the essence of them to you.

The *Pivoting Process* Can Reorient My Life

The *Process of Pivoting* is a conscious recognition that every subject is really two subjects, and then a deliberate speaking or thinking about the *desired* aspect of the subject. *Pivoting* will help you activate within yourself the aspects that you desire regarding all subjects; and once you accomplish that, the essence of the things that you desire, on all subjects, must come into your experience.

There is an important clarification that we must make here: If you are using words that speak of something that you desire while at the same time you are feeling *doubt* about your own words, your *words* are not bringing you what you want, because the way you are *feeling* is the true indication of the creative direction of your thought-vibration. *The Law of Attraction is not responding to your words but to the vibration that is emanating from you.*

However, since you cannot speak of what you *do* want and what you *do not* want at the same time, the more you speak of what you *do* want, the less frequently you will be speaking of what you *do not* want. And if you are serious about telling it like you want it to be rather than like it is, you will, in time (and usually a rather short time), change the balance of your vibration. If you speak it often enough, you will come to feel what you speak.

But there is something even more significantly powerful about this *Process of Pivoting: When life seems to have you negatively oriented toward the lack of something you want, and when you make the statement "I know what I do not want; what is it that I do want?" the answer to that question is summoned from within you, and in that very moment the beginning of a vibrational shift occurs. Pivoting is a powerful tool that will instantly improve your life.*

I Am the Creator of My Life Experience

You are the creator of your own life experience, and as the creator of your experience, it is important to understand that it is not by virtue of your action, not by virtue of your doing—it is not even by virtue of what you are saying—that you are creating. You are creating by virtue of the thought that you are offering.

You cannot speak or offer action without thought-vibration occurring at the same time; however, you are often offering a thought-vibration without offering words or action. Children or babies learn to mimic the vibration of the adults who surround them long before they learn to mimic their words.

Every thought that you think has its own vibrational frequency. Each thought that you offer, whether it has come to you out of your memory, whether it is an influence from another, or whether it is a thought that has become the combination of something *you* have been thinking and something that *another* has been thinking— every thought that you are pondering in your *now*—is vibrating at a very personal frequency . . . and by the powerful *Law of Attraction* (the essence of that which is like unto itself, is drawn), that thought is now attracting another thought that is its Vibrational Match. And now, those combined thoughts are vibrating at a frequency that is higher than the thought that came before; and they will now, by the *Law of Attraction,* attract another and another and another, until eventually the thoughts will be powerful enough to attract a "real life" situation or manifestation.

All people, circumstances, events, and situations are attracted to you by the power of the thoughts that you are thinking. Once you understand that you are literally thinking or vibrating things into being, you may discover a new resolve within you to more deliberately direct your own thoughts.

Aligned Thoughts Are Thoughts That Feel Good

Many people believe that there is more to their Beingness than what is represented in their physical reality as the flesh, blood, and bone person they know themselves to be. As people grapple with ways to label this larger part of themselves, they use words such as *Soul, Source,* or *God.* We refer to that larger, older, wiser part of you as your *Inner Being,* but the label that you choose to describe this Eternal part of you is not important. What is extremely significant is that you understand that the larger *You* does, and will eternally, exist and plays a very large part in the experience that you are living here on planet Earth.

Every thought, word, or deed that you offer is played against the backdrop of that Broader Perspective. Indeed, the reason that in any moment of clearly knowing what you *do not* want, you emphatically then realize what it is that you *do* want is because that larger part of you is giving its undivided attention to what you *do* want.

As you make a conscious effort to guide your thoughts, day by day, more in the direction of what you *do* want, you will begin to feel better and better because the vibration that is activated by your improved-feeling thought will be a closer match to the vibration of the larger Non-Physical part of you. Your desire to think thoughts that feel good will guide you into alignment with the Broader Perspective of your *Inner Being.* In fact, it is not possible for you to really feel good in any moment unless the thoughts you are thinking right now are a Vibrational Match to the thoughts of your *Inner Being.*

For example, your *Inner Being* focuses upon your value—when you identify some flaw in yourself, the negative emotion that you feel is about that vibrational discord or resistance. Your *Inner Being* chooses to focus only upon things about which it can feel love—when you are focusing upon some aspect of someone or something that you abhor, you have focused yourself out of vibrational alignment with your *Inner Being.* Your *Inner Being* focuses only upon your success—when you choose to see something you are doing as failure, you are out of alignment with the perspective of your *Inner Being.*

Seeing My World Through the Eyes of Source

By choosing better-feeling thoughts and by speaking more of what you *do* want and less of what you *do not* want, you will gently tune yourself to the vibrational frequency of your broader, wiser *Inner Being.* To be in vibrational alignment with that Broader Perspective while living your own physical life experience is truly the best of all worlds because as you achieve vibrational alignment with that Broader Perspective, you then see your world from that Broader Perspective. *To see your world through the eyes of Source is truly the most spectacular view of life, for from that vibrational vantage point, you are in alignment with—and therefore in the process of attracting— only what you would consider to be the very best of your world.*

Esther, the woman who translates the vibration of Abraham into the spoken or written word, does so by relaxing and deliberately allowing the vibration of her own Being to raise until it harmonizes with the Non-Physical vibration of Abraham. She has been doing this for many years now, and it has become a very natural thing for her to do. She has long understood the advantage of aligning her vibration so that she could effectively translate our knowledge for other physical friends, but she had not really understood another wonderful benefit of that alignment until one beautiful spring morning when she walked down the driveway by herself to open the gate for her mate, who would eventually follow in the automobile.

As she stood there waiting, she gazed up into the sky and found it to be more beautiful than it had ever appeared before: It was rich in color, and the contrast of the brilliant blue sky and the strikingly white clouds was amazing to her. She could hear the sweet songs of birds that were so far away she could not see them, but their beautiful sound made her shiver with excitement as she heard them. They sounded as if they were right above her head or sitting on her shoulder. And then she became aware of many different delicious fragrances flowing from plants and flowers and earth, moving in the wind and enveloping her. She felt alive and happy and in love with her beautiful world. And she said right out loud, "There can never have been, in all of the Universe, a more beautiful moment in time than this, right here, right now!"

And then she said, "Abraham, it is *you*, isn't it?" And we smiled a very broad smile through her lips, for she had caught us peeping through her eyes, hearing through her ears, smelling through her nose, feeling through her skin.

"Indeed," we said, "we are enjoying the deliciousness of your physical world through your physical body."

Those moments in your life when you feel absolute exhilaration are moments of complete alignment with the Source within you. Those moments when you feel powerful attraction to an idea, or keen interest, are also moments of complete alignment. In fact, the better you feel, the more in alignment you are with your Source— with *who-you-really-are.*

This alignment with your Broader Perspective will not only allow you faster achievement of the big things that you want in life—like wonderful relationships, satisfying careers, and the resources to do the things you really want to do—but this conscious alignment will enhance every moment of your day. *As you tune yourself to the perspective of your Inner Being, your days will be filled with wonderful moments of clarity, satisfaction, and love. And that is truly the way you intended to live while here in this wonderful place, this wonderful time, and this wonderful body.*

I Can Deliberately Choose to Feel Better

The reason that Esther was able to allow that fuller perspective of Abraham to flow through her, providing her with such a delicious experience, was because she had begun that day by looking for reasons to feel good. She looked for the first thing to feel good about while she was still lying in her bed, and that good-feeling thought attracted another and another and another and another and another, until by the time she reached the gate (which was approximately two hours later), by virtue of her *deliberate* choice of thoughts, she had brought her vibrational frequency to a level that was close enough to matching that of her *Inner Being* that her *Inner Being* was able to easily interact with her.

Not only does the thought you are choosing right now attract the next thought and the next . . . and so on—it also provides the basis of your alignment with your Inner Being. As you consistently and deliberately think and speak more of what you do want and less of what you do not want, you will find yourself more often in alignment with the pure, positive essence of your own Source; and under those conditions, your life will be extremely pleasing to you.

Could Illness Be Caused by Negative Emotion?

Esther's experience at the gate was dramatically enhanced by her vibrational alignment with her Source and therefore with absolute Well-Being. But it is also possible for you to experience the opposite of that enhanced experience if you are *out* of alignment with Source and Well-Being. In other words, sickness or illness, or lack of Well-Being, occurs when you vibrationally disallow your alignment with Well-Being.

Whenever you experienced *negative emotion (fear, doubt, frustration, loneliness,* and so on), that feeling of negative emotion was the result of your thinking a thought that did not vibrate at a frequency that was in harmony with your *Inner Being.* Through all of your life experiences—physical and Non-Physical—your *Inner Being,* or the *Total You,* has evolved to a place of *knowing.* And so, whenever you are consciously focused upon a thought that does not harmonize with that which your *Inner Being* has come to know—the resultant feeling within you will be one of negative emotion.

If you were to sit on your foot and cut off the circulation of the flow of blood, or if you were to put a tourniquet around your neck and restrict the flow of oxygen, you would feel immediate evidence of the restriction. And, in like manner, when you think thoughts that are not in harmony with the thoughts of your *Inner Being,* the flow of *Life Force,* or *Energy,* that comes into your physical body is stifled or restricted—and the result of that restriction is that you feel negative emotion. *When you allow that negative emotion to continue over a long period of time, you often experience deterioration of your physical body.*

Remember, every subject is really two subjects: *what is wanted* or *lack of what is wanted.* It is like picking up a stick with two ends: One end represents what you *do* want; the other end represents what you *do not* want. So the stick called "Physical Well-Being" has "wellness" on one end and "illness" on the other. However, people do not experience "illness" only because they are looking at the negative end of the "Physical Well-Being" stick, but because they have been looking at the "I know what I *don't* want" end of many, *many* sticks.

When *your* chronic attention is upon things that you *do not* want—while the chronic attention of your *Inner Being* is upon the things that you *do* want—over time, you cause a vibrational separation between you and your *Inner Being,* and that is what all illness is: separation (caused by your choice of thoughts) between *you* and your *Inner Being.*

Pivot from Feeling Bad to Feeling Good

Everyone wants to feel good, but most people believe that everything around them needs to be pleasing to them *before* they can feel good. In fact, most people feel the way they do in any moment in time because of something they are observing. If what they are observing pleases them, they feel good, but if what they are observing does not please them, they feel bad. Most people feel quite powerless about consistently feeling good because they believe that in order to feel good, the conditions around them must change, but they also believe that they do not have the power to change many of the conditions.

However, once you understand that every subject really is two subjects—what is wanted and lack of it—you can learn to see more of the positive aspects of whatever you are giving your attention to. *That really is all that the Process of Pivoting is: deliberately looking for a more positive way—a better-feeling way—to approach whatever you are giving your attention to.*

When you are facing an unwanted condition and are therefore feeling bad, if you will deliberately say, "I know what I *do not* want . . . what is it that I *do* want?" the vibration of your Being, which is affected by your point of focus, will shift slightly, causing your point of attraction to shift, also. This is the way that you begin telling a different story about your life. Rather than saying, "I never have enough money," you say instead, "I'm looking forward to having more money." That is a very different story—a very different vibration and a very different feeling, which will, in time, bring you a very different result.

As you continue to ask yourself, from your ever-changing vantage point, "What is it that I do want?" eventually you will be standing in a very pleasing place—for you cannot continually ask yourself what it is that you do want without your point of attraction beginning to shift in that direction. . . . The process will be gradual, but your continued application of the process will yield wonderful results in only a few days.

Am I in Harmony with My Desire?

So the *Pivoting Process* is simply: Whenever you recognize that you are feeling a negative emotion (it is really that you are feeling the lack of harmony with something that you want), the obvious thing for you to do is to stop and say, *I'm feeling negative emotion, which means I am not in harmony with something that I want. What do I want?*

Anytime that you are feeling negative emotion, you are in a very good position to identify what it is that you are, in that moment, wanting—because never are you clearer about what you *do want* than when you are experiencing what you *do not want*. And so, stop, in that moment, and say: *Something is important here; otherwise, I would not be feeling this negative emotion. What is it that I want?* And then simply turn your attention to what you do want. *. . . In the moment you turn your attention to what you want, the negative attraction will stop; and in the moment the negative attraction stops, the positive attraction will begin. And—in that moment—your feeling will change from not feeling good to feeling good. That is the* <u>*Process of Pivoting.*</u>

What Do I Want, and *Why?*

Perhaps the strongest resistance that people have to beginning to tell a different story about their own life is their belief that they should always speak "the truth" about where they are or that they should "tell it like it is." But when you understand that the *Law of Attraction* is responding to you while you are telling your story of "how it is"—and therefore is perpetuating more of whatever story you are telling—you may decide that it really is in your best interest to tell a different story, a story that more closely matches what you would *now* like to live. When you acknowledge what you *do not* want, and then ask yourself, "What is it that I *do* want?" you begin a gradual shift into the telling of your new story and into a much-improved point of attraction.

It is always helpful to remember that you get the essence of what you think about—whether you want it or not—because the <u>*Law of Attraction*</u> *is unerringly consistent. Therefore, you are never only telling the story of "how it is now." You are also telling the story of the future experience that you are creating right now.*

Sometimes people misunderstand what the *Process of Pivoting* is, as they incorrectly assume that *to pivot* means to look at something *unwanted* and try to convince themselves that it *is* wanted. They think that we are asking them to look at something that they clearly believe is *wrong* and to pronounce it *right,* or that it is a way of kidding themselves into accepting some unwanted thing. But you are never in a position where you can *kid* yourself into feeling better about something, because the way you feel is the way you feel, and the way you feel is always a result of the thought that you have chosen.

It is really a wonderful thing that, through the process of living life and noticing the things around you that you *do not want,* you are then able to come to clear conclusions about what you *do* want. And when you care about how you feel, you can easily apply the *Process of Pivoting* to direct your attention toward more of the *wanted* aspects, and less of the *unwanted* aspects, of life. And then, as the *Law of Attraction* responds to your increasingly improved, better-feeling thoughts, you will notice your own life experience transforming to match more of those *wanted* aspects, while the *unwanted* aspects gradually fade out of your experience.

When you deliberately apply the <u>Process of Pivoting,</u> *which means you are deliberately choosing your own thoughts, which means you are deliberately choosing your vibrational point of attraction, you are also deliberately choosing how your life unfolds.* <u>Pivoting</u> *is the process of deliberately focusing your attention with the intent of directing your own life experience.*

I Can Feel Better Right Now

People often complain that it would be much easier for them to focus on something positive if it were already happening in their life experience. They accurately acknowledge that it is much easier to feel good about something when something good is already happening. We certainly do not disagree that it is easier to feel good while noticing things you believe are good. But if you believe that you only have the ability to focus upon what *is* happening, and if what *is* happening is not pleasing, then you could wait an entire lifetime because your attention to *unwanted* things is preventing *wanted* things from coming to you.

You do not have to wait for a good thing to happen in order to feel good, for you have the ability to direct your thoughts toward improved things no matter what is currently present in your experience. And when you care about how you feel and you are willing to pivot and turn your attention toward better-feeling thoughts, you will quickly begin the positive, deliberate transformation of your life.

Things that are coming into your experience are coming in response to your vibration. Your vibration is offered because of the thoughts you are thinking, and you can tell by the way you feel what kinds of thoughts you are thinking. Find good-feeling thoughts and good-feeling manifestations must follow.

Many people say, "It would be so much easier for me to be happy if I were in a different place: if my relationship were better, if my mate were easier to live with, if my physical body didn't hurt or if my body looked different, if my work was more fulfilling, if I only had more money. . . . If the conditions of my life were better, I would feel better, and then it would be easier for me to be thinking more positive thoughts."

Seeing pleasing things does feel good, and it is easier to feel good when a pleasing thing is there, obvious for you to see—but you cannot ask others around you to orchestrate only pleasing things for you to see. Expecting others to provide the perfect environment for you is not a good idea, for many reasons: (1) It is not their responsibility to feather your nest; (2) it is not possible for them to control conditions you have created around you; and (3) most important of all, you would be giving up your power to create your own experience.

Make a decision to look for the best-feeling aspects of whatever you must give your attention to, and otherwise look only for good-feeling things to give your attention to—and your life will become one of increasingly good-feeling aspects.

Attention to Unwanted Attracts More Unwanted

For every pleasing thing, there is an unpleasing counterpart, for within every particle of the Universe is that which is wanted as well as the lack of that which is wanted. When you focus upon an unwanted aspect of something in an effort to push it away from you, instead it only comes closer, because you get what you give your attention to whether it is something that you want or not.

You live in a Universe that is based on "inclusion." In other words, there is no such thing as "exclusion" in this "inclusion-based" Universe. When you see something that you desire and you say yes to it, that is the equivalent of saying, "Yes, this thing that I desire, please *come to me.*" When you see something that you do not want and you shout no at it, that is the equivalent of saying, *"Come to me,* this thing that I do not want!"

Within everything that surrounds you is *that which is wanted* and *that which is unwanted.* It is up to you to focus upon what is wanted. See your environment as a buffet of many choices, and make more deliberate choices about what you think about. If you will try to make choices that feel good to you, as you make an effort to tell a different story about your life and the people and experiences that are in it, you will see your life begin to transform to match the essence of the details of the new-and-improved story you are now telling.

Am I Focused upon the Wanted or the Unwanted?

Sometimes you believe that you are focused upon what you want when actually the opposite is true. Just because your words sound positive, or your lips are smiling while you say them, does not mean that you are vibrating on the positive end of the stick. It is only by being aware of the way you are *feeling* while offering your words that you can be sure that you are, in fact, offering a vibration about what you *do* want, rather than what you *do not* want.

Focus on the Solution, Not the Problem

In the midst of what the television weatherman was calling "a serious drought," our friend Esther walked down one of the paths on their Texas Hill Country property, noticing the dryness of the grass and feeling real concern for the well-being of the beautiful trees and bushes that were all beginning to show signs of stress from the shortage of rain. She noticed that the birdbath was empty even though she had filled it with water just a few hours earlier, and then she thought about the thirsty deer who had probably jumped the fence to drink the small amount of water that it held. And so, as she was pondering the direness of the situation, she stopped, looked upward, and—in a very positive voice, with very positive-sounding words—said, "Abraham, I want some rain."

And we said immediately back to her, "Indeed, from this position of lack, you think you will get rain?"

"What am I doing wrong?" she asked.

And we asked, *"Why* do you want the rain?"

And Esther answered, "I want it because it refreshes the earth. I want it because it gives all of the creatures in the bushes water so that they have enough to drink. I want it because it makes the grass green, and it feels good upon my skin, and it makes us all feel better."

And we said, "Now, you are attracting rain."

Our question *"Why* do you want the rain?" helped Esther withdraw her attention from the *problem* and turn her attention toward the *solution.* When you consider *why* you want something, your vibration usually shifts or *pivots* in the direction of your desire. Whenever you consider *how* it will happen, or *when,* or *who* will bring it, your vibration usually then shifts back toward the problem.

You see, in the process of taking her attention from what was wrong—by our asking her *why* she wanted the rain—she accomplished a *pivot.* She began thinking not only of *what* she wanted, but *why* she wanted it; and in the process, she began to feel better. That afternoon it rained, and that night the local weatherman reported "an unusual isolated thunderstorm in the Hill Country."

Your thoughts are powerful, and you have much more control over your own experience than most of you realize.

What I *Do* Want Is to Feel Good

A young father found himself at his wit's end because his young son was wetting the bed every night. Not only was this father frustrated about the physical disruption of finding wet bedding and clothing every morning, but he was concerned about the emotional ramifications of this continuing for such a long time. And, frankly, he was embarrassed by his son's behavior. "He's too big for this," he complained to us.

We asked, "When you come into the bedroom in the morning, what happens?"

"Well, as soon as I walk into his room, I can tell by the odor that he has wet the bed again," he answered.

"And how do you feel at that point?" we asked.

"Helpless, angry, frustrated. This has been going on for a long time, and I don't know what to do about it."

"What do you say to your son?"

"I tell him to get out of those wet clothes and get into the bathtub. I tell him he's too big for this and that we've talked about it before."

We told this father that he was actually perpetuating bed-wetting. We explained: *When the way you feel is controlled by a condition, you can never influence a change in the condition; but when you are able to control the way you feel within a condition, then you have the power to influence change in the condition.* For example, when you enter your son's bedroom and become aware that something that you do not want to happen has happened, if you would stop for a moment to acknowledge the thing that has happened that you *do not want*—asking yourself what it is that you *do* want and then further enforcing that side of the pivotal equation by asking yourself *why* you want it—not only would *you* immediately feel better, but you would soon begin to see the results of your positive influence.

"What *do* you want?" we asked.

He said, "I want my little one to wake up happy and dry and proud of himself and not to be embarrassed."

This father felt relief as he focused upon what he wanted because in making that effort, he found harmony with his desire. We told him, "As you are thinking those sorts of thoughts, then what will be oozing out of you will be in harmony with what you *do* want rather than in harmony with what you *do not* want, and you will be more positively influencing your son. Then words will come out of you such as: 'Oh, this is part of growing up. All of us have been through this, and you are growing up very fast. Now get out of those wet clothes and get into the bathtub.'" This young father called very soon after that and happily reported that the bed-wetting had stopped. . . .

Whenever I'm Feeling Bad, I'm Attracting Unwanted

While almost everyone is aware of how they feel in varying degrees, there are few who understand the important guidance that their feelings or emotions provide. In the most simple of terms: *Whenever you feel bad, you are in the process of attracting something that will not please you. Without exception, the reason for negative emotion is because you are focused upon something you do not want or upon the lack or absence of something that you do want.*

Many regard negative emotion as something unwanted, but we prefer to see it as important guidance to help you to understand the direction of your focus . . . therefore, the direction of your vibration . . . therefore, the direction of what you are attracting. You could call it a "warning bell," because it certainly does give you a signal to let you know that it is time to pivot, but we prefer to call it a *"guiding* bell."

Your emotions are your *Guidance System* to assist you in understanding what you are in the process of creating with every thought you think. Often people who are beginning to understand the power of thought and the importance of focusing upon good-feeling subjects are embarrassed or even angry at themselves when they find themselves in the midst of negative emotion, but there is no reason to be angry at yourself for having a perfectly functioning *Guidance System.*

Whenever you become aware that you are feeling negative emotion, begin by complimenting yourself for being aware of your Guidance, and then gently try to improve the feeling by choosing thoughts that feel better. We would call this a very subtle <u>Process of Pivoting</u> whereby you gently choose better-feeling thoughts.

Whenever you feel negative emotion, you could say to yourself, *I'm feeling some negative emotion, which means I'm in the process of attracting something that I do not want. What is it that I <u>do</u> want?*

Often just acknowledging that you "want to feel good" will help turn your thoughts in a better-feeling direction. But it is important to understand the distinction between "*wanting* to feel good" and "not *wanting* to feel bad." Some people think that it is just two different ways of saying the same thing, when actually those statements are exact opposites, with huge vibrational differences. *If you can begin to orient your thoughts by steadily looking for things that cause you to feel good, you will begin to develop patterns of thoughts, or beliefs, that will help you create magnificent, good-feeling lives.*

My Thoughts Dovetail into Stronger Matching Thoughts

Whatever thought you are focused upon—whether it is a memory from your past, something you are observing in your present, or something you are anticipating in your future—that thought is active within you right now, and it is attracting other thoughts and ideas that are similar. Not only do your thoughts attract other thoughts that are of a similar nature, but the longer you focus, the stronger the thoughts become and the more attraction power they amass.

Our friend Jerry likened this to the ropes he once observed while watching a large ship being docked. It was to be tied with a rope that was very large—too big and bulky to be thrown across the expanse of water. And so, instead, a small ball of twine was tossed across the water to the dock. The twine had been spliced into a little bigger rope, which had been spliced into a little bigger rope, which had been spliced into a little bigger rope . . . until eventually, the very large rope could be easily pulled across the expanse of water, and the ship was then secured to the dock. This is similar to the way your thoughts dovetail into one another, with one connecting to another, connecting to another, and so on.

Upon some subjects, because you have been pulling on the negative rope longer, it is very easy for you to get off on a negative tangent. In other words, it just takes a little negative utterance from someone, a memory of something, or some suggestion that takes you into a negative tailspin right away.

Your point of attraction predominantly occurs from the day-to-day things that you are thinking as you are moving through your day, and you have the power to direct your thoughts positively or negatively. For example: You are in the grocery store, and you notice that something that you regularly purchase has increased substantially in price, and you feel strong discomfort wash over you. You may very well think that you are just feeling shock over the sudden spike in the price of this item, and that since you have no say in what the grocer charges for any of the items in this store, you have no option other than to feel discomfort about it. However, we want to point out that your feeling of discomfort is not because of the grocer's action of raising the price of the goods for sale, but instead it is because of the direction of your own thoughts.

Just like the analogy of the rope tied to the rope tied to the rope tied to the rope, your thoughts are tied to one another and travel quickly to heightened vibrational places. For example, *Wow, the price of this is much greater than it was just last week . . . this price jump seems unreasonable . . . there's nothing reasonable about the greed in the marketplace . . . things are getting way out of hand . . . I don't know where it's all headed . . . it doesn't seem like we can go on like this . . . our economy is in trouble . . . I can't afford these inflated prices . . . I'm having a hard time making ends meet . . . I can't seem to earn it fast enough to keep up with the increase in the cost of living. . . .*

And, of course, this negative train of thought could move in many directions—toward blame of the grocer, to the economy, to your government—but it usually always turns back to the way you feel that the situation will negatively impact you, because everything that you observe feels personal to you. And everything, in truth, *is* personal to you because you are offering a vibration about it that is affecting what now is being attracted to you by your choice of thoughts.

If you are aware of how you are feeling and you understand that your emotions are indicating the direction of your thoughts, then you can more deliberately guide your thoughts. For example: *Wow, the price of this is much greater than it was just last week . . . however, I'm not aware of the other items in my basket . . . they could be the same . . . or maybe even a bit lower . . . I wasn't really paying attention . . . this one just got my attention because it was so much greater . . . prices do fluctuate . . . I always manage . . . things are going up a bit, but it's working out all right . . . it is quite an impressive system of distribution that makes this variety of goods so accessible to us. . . .*

Once you decide that you care about feeling good, you will find it easier to more consistently choose a better-feeling direction in your thoughts.

When the desire to feel good is effectively active within you, a consistent inspiration toward good-feeling thoughts will be present, and you will find it easier and easier to direct your thoughts in productive directions. Your thoughts contain enormous creative, attractive power that you harness effectively only by consistently offering good-feeling thoughts. When your thoughts constantly move back and forth between wanted and unwanted, pros and cons, pluses and minuses—you lose the benefit of the momentum of your pure, positive thought.

Creating a *Book of Positive Aspects*

In the first year of Jerry and Esther's work with us, they were using small hotel meeting rooms in different cities within 300 miles of their home in Texas to provide a comfortable place where people could gather to address their personal questions with us. There was a hotel in the city of Austin that always seemed to forget they were coming even though Esther had made arrangements with the hotel, signed contracts, and even called in the days just prior to the event to confirm. The hotel was always able to accommodate them (even though when they arrived, no one seemed to be expecting them), but it was very uncomfortable for Jerry and Esther to be in the position of urging the hotel staff to hurry to get the room ready before their guests arrived.

Finally, Esther said, "I think we should find a new hotel."

And we said, "That might be a good idea, but remember, *you will take yourselves with you.*"

"What do you mean?" Esther asked, a bit defensively.

We explained, *"If you take action from your perspective of lack— the action is always counterproductive.* In fact, it is likely that the new hotel will treat you just like the last one did." Jerry and Esther laughed at our explanation because they had already moved from one hotel to another for the very same reason.

"What should we do?" they asked. We encouraged them to purchase a new notebook and write boldly across the front cover of it: My Book of Positive Aspects. And on the first page of the book, write: "Positive Aspects of the _____ Hotel in Austin."

And so, Esther began to write: "It is a beautiful facility. It is immaculate. It is well situated. Very close to the interstate, with easy-to-find directions. There are many different-sized rooms to accommodate our increasing numbers. The hotel staff is always very friendly. . . ."

As Esther was making those entries, her *feeling* about the hotel changed from one of negative to one of positive, and in the moment that she began to *feel* better, her *attraction* from the hotel changed.

She did not write: "They are always ready and waiting for us," because that had not been her experience, and writing that would have evoked a feeling of contradiction or a feeling of defense or justification from her. By wanting to feel good, and by deliberately focusing her attention more upon the things about the hotel that did feel good, Esther's point of attraction regarding this hotel shifted, and then something Esther found very interesting happened: The hotel never forgot they were coming again. Esther was amused to realize that the hotel had not been forgetting about their agreement because they were uncaring or disorganized. The hotel staff was simply being influenced by Esther's dominant thought about them. In short, they could not buck the current of Esther's negative thought.

Esther enjoyed her *Book of Positive Aspects* so much that she began writing pages on many subjects of her life. We encouraged her to not only write about the things in which she was seeking improved feelings, but to write about things she already felt mostly positive about, just to get in the habit of good-feeling thoughts and for the pleasure of good-feeling thoughts. It is a nice way to live.

The *Law of Attraction* Adds Power to Thoughts

Often, when experiencing an unwanted situation, you feel a need to explain why it has happened, in an attempt, perhaps, to justify why you are in the situation. *Whenever you are defending or justifying or rationalizing or blaming anything or anyone, you remain in a place of negative attraction.* Every word you speak as you explain why something is not the way you want it to be continues the negative attraction, for you cannot be focused upon what you *do* want while you are explaining *why* you are experiencing something that you *do not* want. *You cannot be focused upon negative aspects and positive aspects at the same time.*

Often, in an effort to determine where your trouble started, you only hold yourself in that negative attraction longer: *What is the source of my trouble? What is the reason that I'm not where I want to be?* It is natural that you want improvement in your experience, and therefore it is logical that you are solution oriented . . . but there is a big difference between seriously looking for a solution and justifying the need for a solution by emphasizing the problem.

The realization that something is not as you want it to be is an important first step, but once you have identified that, the faster you are able to turn your attention in the direction of a solution, the better, because a continuing exploration of the problem will prevent you from finding the solution. The problem is a different vibrational frequency than the solution.

As you become aware of the value of the *Process of Pivoting,* and you become adept at identifying what is not wanted and then immediately turning your attention toward what is wanted, you will realize that you are surrounded primarily by wonderful things, for there is so much more that is going right in your world than wrong. Also, a daily utilization of the *Book of Positive Aspects* will help you to become more positively oriented. It will assist you in gradually tipping the balance of your thoughts more in the direction of what you *do* want.

The more that you focus your attention with the intention of finding increasingly *better-feeling* thoughts, the more you will realize that there is a very big difference between thinking about what you want and thinking about the absence of it. Whenever you are feeling uncomfortable as you are speaking or thinking about improving something you want—such as a better financial condition or an improved relationship or physical condition—you are in that moment preventing yourself from finding the improvement.

The *Process of Pivoting* and the *Process of the Book of Positive Aspects* are both being offered to assist you in recognizing—in the early, subtle stages of your creation—that you are pulling on the very tips of that negative ball of twine, so that you may, right away, release it and reach for the positive thread of thought.

It is much easier to go from a thought of something that makes you feel a little better, to an even better-feeling thought, to an even better-feeling thought . . . than to go directly to a wonderful-feeling thought, because all thoughts (or vibrations) are affected by (or managed by) the <u>*Law of Attraction.*</u>

I'll Begin My Day with Good-Feeling Thoughts

When you are focused upon something that you really do not want, it is actually easier for you to remain focused upon that unwanted topic (even finding other evidence to support that thought) than it is to move to a more positive perspective, because *thoughts that are like unto themselves, are drawn.* So if you attempt to make a big jump from a truly negative, unwanted topic immediately to a positive, delightful topic of something very much wanted, you will not be able to make the jump—for there is too much vibrational disparity between the two thoughts. A determination to gently, generally, and steadily lean more and more in the direction of wanted things is really the best way to approach your personal vibrational improvement.

When you first awaken in the morning, after a few hours of sleep (and therefore a vibrational detachment from unwanted things), you are in your most positive vibrational state. If you would begin your day, even before you get out of bed, by looking for a handful of positive aspects in your life, you will begin your day in a more positive vein, and the thoughts that the *Law of Attraction* will now provide as your springboard into each day will be much better feeling and beneficial.

In other words, every morning you have an opportunity to establish another vibrational basis (a sort of set-point) that sets the general tone of your thoughts for the rest of the day. And while it is possible that some events of your day may deviate from that starting place, in time you will see that you have established complete control of your thoughts, your vibration, your point of attraction—your life!

Sleep Time Is Realignment-of-Energies Time

While you are sleeping—or during the time that you are not consciously focused through your physical body—the attraction to this physical body stops. Sleep is a time when your *Inner Being* can realign your Energies, and it is a time for refreshment and replenishment of your physical body. If, when you put yourself in your bed, you will say, *Tonight I will rest well—I know that all attraction to this body will stop and when I awaken in the morning, I will literally reemerge back into my physical experience,* you will receive the greatest benefit from your time of sleep.

Awaking in the morning is not so different from being born. It is not so different from the day you first emerged into your physical body. So, as you awaken, open your eyes and say, *Today, I will look for reasons to feel good. Nothing is more important than that I feel good. Nothing is more important than that I choose thoughts that attract other thoughts that attract other thoughts that raise my vibrational frequency to the place where I can resonate with the positive aspects of the Universe.*

ur vibration is right where you last left it. So if you lie in your
worrying about a situation before you go to sleep, when you
awaken, you will pick up right where your thoughts or vibration
left off the night before, and then your thoughts for the day will
get off on that negative footing. And then the *Law of Attraction*
will continue to serve up for you other thoughts that are like those
thoughts. But if you will make an effort as you go to sleep to identify some of the positive aspects of your life, and then deliberately
release your thoughts as you remember that during your slumber
you are going to detach and refresh, and then if, when you awaken,
you will open your eyes and say, *Today, I will look for reasons to feel
good* . . . you will begin to gain control of your thoughts and life.

Rather than worrying about the problems of the world, or
thinking about the things that you have to do today, just lie in your
bed and look for the positive aspects of the moment: *How wonderful this bed feels. How comforting the fabric feels. How good my body
feels. How comfortable this pillow is. How refreshing the air is that I'm
breathing. How good it is to be alive!* . . . You will have begun to pull
on that positive, good-feeling rope.

The *Law of Attraction* is like a giant magnifying glass amplifying whatever is. And so, as you awaken and look for some reason
(something very immediate to you) to feel good about, the *Law of
Attraction* will then offer you another thought that feels like it, and
then another, and then another—and that is really what we call
getting out of bed on the right foot.

With a little bit of effort, and a desire to feel good, you can
direct your thoughts to more and more pleasing scenarios until
you will change your habits of thoughts as well as your point of
attraction—and the evidence of your improvement in thoughts will
begin to show up right away.

An Example of a *Positive Aspects Bedtime Process*

Your action orientation in life causes you to believe that it takes
hard work to make things happen, but as you learn to deliberately
direct your thoughts, you will discover that there is tremendous

leverage and power in thought. As you focus more consistently only in the direction of what you desire rather than diluting the power of your thought by thinking of the *wanted,* and then the *unwanted,* you will understand, from your personal experience, what we mean. Because of your *action* orientation, you often try too hard and work too hard. And as a result of that, most of you bring yourselves more to the attention of what is wrong (or more to the attention of what needs to be fixed) than you do to the attention of what you desire.

Here is a good way to apply the *Process of Positive Aspects* at bedtime: Once you are in your bed, try to recall some of the most pleasant things that happened during the day. Since many things have undoubtedly happened during this day, you may have to ponder for a little while, and you may remember some less-than-pleasant things that happened—but stick to your intention of finding something pleasing, and when you find it, ponder it.

Prime your positive pump by saying things such as: *The thing I liked about that was. . . . My favorite part of that was. . . .* Follow any positive thread that you find, thinking about the best parts of your day; and then, once you are feeling the effect of your positive thoughts, focus on your dominant intention right now: *getting a good night's sleep and awakening refreshed in the morning.*

Say to yourself, *I'm going to sleep now; and while I am sleeping, because my thoughts will be inactive, attraction will stop and my physical body will be completely refreshed at every level.* Turn your attention to the immediate things around you, like the comfort of your bed, the softness of your pillow, the Well-Being of your moment. And then softly set forth the intention: *I will sleep well, and I will awaken refreshed with another new, good-feeling, positive point of attraction.* And then, off to sleep.

An Example of a *Positive Aspects Morning Process*

As you awaken the next morning, you will be in that positive, good-feeling place, and your first thoughts will be something like: *Ah, I am awake. I have reemerged back into the physical. . . .* Lie there for a little while and bask in the comfort of your bed, and then offer a thought such as: *Today, no matter where I am going, no matter what I am doing, no matter who I'm doing it with, it is my dominant intent to look for things that feel good. When I feel good, I am vibrating with my higher power. When I feel good, I am in harmony with that which I consider to be good. When I feel good, I am in the mode of attracting that which will please me once it gets here. And when I feel good—I feel good!* (It is good just to feel good if the only thing it ever brought to you is the way you feel in the moment—but it brings ever so much more beyond that.)

We would lie in the bed for two or three minutes (that is enough), and we would look for the positive aspects of our surroundings. And then, as we move into the day, we would begin to acknowledge more positive aspects, looking for reasons to feel good no matter what the object of our attention is.

In the first moment of any negative emotion—which very likely will occur even though you have begun your day looking for reasons to feel good because there is, upon some subjects, some negative momentum already in motion—upon the first inclination of any negative emotion, we would stop and say, *I want to feel good. I'm feeling some negative emotion, which means that I'm focused upon something that I do not want. What is it that I want?* And we would turn our attention immediately to that which we want, staying focused upon the new thought, or the positive thought, long enough that we would feel the positive Energy again beginning to flow through our apparatus.

As you move through your day, look for more reasons to laugh and more reasons to have fun. When you want to feel good, you do not take things so seriously; and when you are not taking things so seriously, you are not as likely to notice the lack of things wanted; and when you are not focusing upon the lack of what you desire, you feel better—and when you feel better, you attract more of what you do want . . . and your life just gets better and better.

And then, that night, as you lie in your bed, you will have many wonderful things to ponder as you drift off into your restful, refreshing sleep; and then you will awaken into an even better-feeling new day tomorrow.

I Know How I Want to Feel

Sometimes when you are in the midst of an uncomfortable situation, you struggle to find *any* positive aspects within it. Some things are intolerable; some things are so big and so bad that it does not seem possible for you to find anything positive about them, but that is because you are attempting to take too large of a jump from the awfulness of what you are focused upon to the solution that you desire. In other words, if you want to find an action solution right now that will fix this but you find yourself in a situation where no action that you can take seems appropriate, always remember that while there may not be a positive aspect to your action in this moment—while you may not be able to figure out what to *do* that would make you feel better—*you always know how you want to feel.*

It is a bit like someone saying, "I've just jumped out of an airplane, and I have no parachute. What should I do now?" There are situations where, given the current circumstances, there is no action or thought that, at this point, will make a significant enough difference to change the outcome that is barreling in upon you. And, in the same way that sometimes you cannot find any *action* that will fix things, there is no *thought* that will immediately change it either.

But if you understand the power of your thought and the incredible leverage that consistently good-feeling thoughts provide, and you begin deliberately choosing your thoughts by utilizing the guidance that your feelings or emotions indicate, you can easily transform your life into predominantly good-feeling experiences by focusing upon the improved feeling. *If you are able to find even the smallest feeling of relief in a deliberately chosen thought—your gentle path toward your solution will begin.*

What to <u>do</u> in certain situations may not be clear to you, and you may at times not even be able to identify what it is that you want to <u>have,</u> but there is never a time that you are unable to identify, to some extent, how you want to <u>feel.</u> In other words, you know that you would rather feel happy *than* sad, *refreshed than* tired, *invigorated rather than* enervated. *You know that you would rather feel* productive *than* unproductive, *free than* confined, *growing than* stagnant. . . .

There is not enough action available to compensate for mis-aligned thought, but when you begin to gain control of the way you feel—by more deliberately choosing the direction of your thought—you will discover the powerful leverage in thought. *If you will bring yourself to a more deliberate control of your own thought, you will bring yourself to a more deliberate control of your own life experience.*

Nothing Is More Important Than Feeling Good

Becoming more deliberate about the things you think about is not a difficult thing. You are often particular about what you eat, the vehicle you drive, and the clothes you wear; and being a delib-erate thinker does not require much more deliberate discrimination than that. But learning to deliberately direct your thoughts toward the aspect of the subject that feels best to you will have a much greater impact on the improvement in your life than the choosing of a meal, vehicle, or wardrobe.

Once you read these words and feel your own personal resonance with their meaning and power, you will never again feel negative emotion without realizing that you are receiving important guidance to assist you in guiding your thoughts in a more productive and beneficial direction. In other words, you will never again feel negative emotion and not understand that it means you are in the process of attracting something *unwanted.* A significant thing is happening with you as you are coming into conscious awareness of your emotions and the guidance that they provide, because even in your ignorance of what negative emotion meant, you were still negatively attracting. And so, understanding your emotions now gives you control of your life experience.

Whenever you are feeling less than good, if you will stop and say, *Nothing is more important than that I feel good—I want to find a reason now to feel good,* you will find an improved thought, which will lead to another and another. As you develop the habit of look-ing for good-feeling thoughts, the circumstances that surround you must improve. The *Law of Attraction* demands it. When you feel good, you experience the sensation of doors opening as the Universe is cooperating with you; and when you feel bad, it feels as if the doors are closing and the cooperation stops.

Anytime you feel negative emotion, you are in the mode of resisting something that you want, and that resistance takes its toll on you. It takes its toll on your physical body, and it takes its toll on the amount of wonderful things that you are allowing to come into your experience.

Through your process of living life and noticing things wanted and unwanted, you have created a sort of *Vibrational Escrow,* which, in a sense, holds for you those wanted things you have identified until you become a close enough Vibrational Match to them that you allow yourself a fully manifested receiving of them. But until you find a way to feel good about them even though they have not yet manifested in your experience, it may seem to you that they are on the outside of a door that you cannot open. However, as you begin to look for more positive aspects regarding the things that occupy your thoughts—and as you deliberately choose the more positive end of the stick of possibilities regarding the subjects that dominate your thought processes—that door will open and everything that you desire will flow easily into your experience.

It Gets Better the Better It Gets

When you deliberately seek positive aspects of whatever you are giving your attention to, you, in a sense, tune your vibrational tuner to more positive aspects of everything. And, of course, you could tune yourself negatively as well. Many people struggle in an attitude of self-criticism as a result of negative comparison that has been directed to them from parents or teachers or peers, and there is nothing more detrimental to your ability to positively attract than a negative attitude toward yourself.

So, sometimes by choosing a subject about which you have practiced fewer negative thoughts, you can tune yourself to a better-feeling frequency; and then from that better-feeling place, as you redirect your thoughts toward yourself, you will find more positive aspects about yourself than usual. *Once you find more positive aspects of the world that surrounds you, you will begin to find more positive aspects about yourself. And once that happens, finding more positive aspects about your world will be easier still.*

When you find things about yourself that you do not like, you will find more of those things in others. You say, "The worse it gets, the worse it gets." But as you are deliberately looking for positive aspects in yourself or in others, you will find more of those things: "The better it gets, the better it gets."

We cannot overemphasize the value in looking for positive aspects and focusing upon more of things wanted, because every-thing that comes to you is dependent upon that very simple prem-ise: *You get more and more of what you are thinking about—whether you want it or not.*

My Universe Is Positively and Negatively Balanced

So, you are the creator of your experience. Or you could say that *you are the attractor of your experience.* Creating is not about identifying something wanted and then going after it and captur-ing it. Creating is about focusing upon the subject of desire—tuning your thoughts more precisely to the aspects of the subject that you would like to experience and therefore allowing the *Law of Attraction* to bring it to you.

Whether you are *remembering* something from the past, *imagining* something about the future, or *observing* something from your now, you are offering thought-vibrations that the *Law of Attraction* is responding to. You may refer to your thoughts as *desires* or *beliefs* (a belief is only a thought you continue to think), but whatever you are giving your attention to is establishing your point of attraction.

Because every subject is actually two subjects—*what is wanted* and *the lack of what is wanted*—it is possible to believe that you are positively focused when in fact you are negatively focused. People may say, "I want more money," but what they are actually focused upon is the fact that they do not have as much money as they need. Most people talk most often about their desire to be healthy when they are feeling sick. In other words, their attention to what they *do not* want is what is prompting their remarks about what they *do* want, but in the majority of cases, even though they may be speaking words that seem to indicate that they are focused upon their desire, they are not.

It is only by consciously recognizing how you are feeling while you are speaking that you really know if you are positively or negatively attracting. And while you may not see immediate evidence of what you are in the process of attracting, whatever you are thinking about is amassing matching thoughts, vibrations, and Energies; and eventually the evidence of your attraction will be obvious.

My Universe Responds to My Attention to . . .

Most people believe, or want to believe, that everything in the Universe responds to their words in the same way that other people around them can sometimes be trained to behave. When you tell someone, "Yes, come to me," you expect them to come. When you say, "No, go away from me," you expect them to go. But you live in an attraction-based Universe (an inclusion-based Universe), which simply means there is no such thing as *no*.

When you give your attention to something wanted and you say, "Yes, come to me," you include it in your vibration, and the *Law of Attraction* begins the process of bringing it. But when you look at something unwanted and you say "No, I do not want you—go away!" the Universe brings that, also. *Your attention to it, and therefore your vibrational alignment with it, is what is causing the response—not your words.*

And so, as you say, "Perfect health, I seek you . . . I want you— I bask in the idea of perfect health," you are attracting health. But as you say, "Sickness, I do not want you," you are attracting sickness. As you say, *"No, no, no,"* it is coming closer, closer, closer, because the more you struggle against something that you do not want, the more engulfed in it you become.

People often believe that once they find their perfect mate, or achieve their perfect body weight, or accumulate enough money, *then, once and for all,* they will also find the happiness that they seek . . . but nowhere is there a little corner of something where only positive aspects exist. The perfect balance of the Universe says that positive and negative (wanted and unwanted) exists in all particles of the Universe. When you, as the creator, the chooser, the definer, the decider, look for the positive aspect, that becomes what you live—in *all* aspects of your life. You do not have to wait around for that perfect thing to show itself to you so that you can then have a positive response to it. Instead, you positively train your thoughts and vibrations, and then you become the *attractor* of it, or the *creator* of it.

We would encourage you to begin each day with the statement: *Today—no matter where I go, no matter what I am doing, and no matter who I am doing it with—it is my dominant intent to look for what I am wanting to see.*

Remember, when you awaken in the morning, you are reborn. While you have slumbered, all attraction has stopped. That sequestering away for a few hours of sleep—where your Consciousness is no longer attracting—gives you a refreshing new beginning. And so, unless you wake up in the morning and begin regurgitating what troubled you the day before, it will not trouble you in your new day, in your new birth, in your new beginning.

Decisions to Feel Good Attract Good Feelings

A woman said to us: "I recently found out that I'm going to be attending three or four holiday parties, and as soon as I heard that, I started thinking, *Oh, Mary's going to be there, and she's going to be gorgeous.* I started immediately comparing myself to other people. I'd like to stop doing that and feel good about *me* and just enjoy the parties, no matter who's there. Could you help me apply the processes of *Pivoting* and *Positive Aspects* regarding my self-consciousness. I really don't even want to attend these parties."

We explained: While your feeling of self-consciousness is amplified as you consider your attendance of these parties, neither the party nor Mary is the reason for your discomfort. It often seems complicated to sort out your relationships with other people, even tracing the beginning of these feelings back into your childhood, but there is no value in doing that. You have the ability, from right where you stand, to find positive aspects or negative aspects—to think of the wanted or unwanted—and whether you begin the process right now or several days before you attend your first party, or whether you wait until you are at the party, the work is the same: *Look for things that feel good when you focus upon them.*

Because you have more control over what is activated in your own mind, it is usually much easier to find the positive aspect of a situation before you are standing right in the middle of it. If you do imagine the situation as you want it to be, and you do practice your positive response to the upcoming situation, then when you are at the party you will witness the control that you set into motion days before.

You cannot feel good and bad at the same time. You cannot focus upon wanted and unwanted at the same time. If you have trained your thoughts to what you consider to be good, or wanted before you arrive at a party, the <u>Law of Attraction</u> *will deliver to you things that feel good and are wanted. It really is as simple as that.*

If you want to feel different at these upcoming parties than you have felt at parties in previous years, you must begin telling a different story. The story you have been telling goes something like this: "I'm only invited to these parties because of my relationship with my mate. It really isn't important to anyone that I be there. I'm not really a part of his work environment, and I don't really understand most of the things that they're interested in. I'm an outsider. Mary doesn't feel like an outsider like I do. Her confidence is obvious in the way she dresses and carries herself. I always feel less attractive, less smart, less everything when I am near Mary. I hate feeling like this. I wish I didn't have to go."

Here is an example of an attempt at a better-feeling story: "My mate is well respected at his firm. It's nice that his company occasionally provides an opportunity for people who work there to include their spouses and to get to know one another. No one there expects me to be up to speed with the inner workings of that environment. In fact, this will be a party where they will probably enjoy thinking about other things than their work.

"Life is much larger than what happens at my husband's office. And since I'm never there, I may very well appear to be a breath of fresh air to many of them because I'm not bogged down in the things they're troubled about. Mary seems light and friendly. She's clearly not bogged down in office politics or problems. It's fun to watch her. She's interesting. I wonder where she buys her clothing—they are very pretty things she wears."

You see, it is not necessary that you sort out every insecurity that you have ever felt and use this office party as a means to solve it. Just find something positive to focus upon and feel the benefit of having done so, and in time, Mary will be a nonissue, or maybe a friend. But in any case, it is your decision to make, and your vibrational practice to make it so.

How Can I Not Feel Their Pain?

Our friend Jerry asked of us: "It seems to me that the majority of my discomfort is felt because I'm observing others who are in pain. How could I use the *Pivoting Process* to not feel pain about *their* pain?"

We explained: Whatever the subject of your attention, it contains things you want to see as well as things you do not want to see. The pain you are feeling is not because the person you are observing is in pain. Your pain is because you have chosen to look at an aspect of them that causes you to feel pain. There is a big difference.

Of course, if this person were not feeling pain but were instead joyful, it would be easier for you to feel joyful, but you must not rely on conditions changing in order to control the way you feel. You must improve your ability to focus positively regardless of the condition—and to do that, it helps to remember that every subject has *wanted* and *unwanted* within it, and that, if you are deliberate, you *can* find something that feels better.

Of course, it is easier just to observe something that is right before your eyes than it is to deliberately sift for things that you would prefer to see. However, when it really matters to you that you feel good, you will be less willing to merely lazily or sloppily observe, for your desire to feel good will inspire a greater willingness to look for positive aspects. Also, the more often you do look for good-feeling things to focus upon, the more of those kinds of good-feeling things the *Law of Attraction* will bring to you, until in time you will be so positively oriented that you simply will not notice the things that don't match your positive orientation.

A mother once said to us, in response to our advising her to ignore her son's problems, "But won't he feel like I've abandoned him? Shouldn't I be there for him?"

We explained to her that there is no "abandonment" in focusing upon the positive aspects of her son's life, and there is powerful value in abandoning *any* thoughts that do not feel good when you think them. We said, "You never help anyone by being their sounding board for problems or complaints. By holding an image of improvement in your son's life, you help him move toward that. Be *there* for him. And call him *there* to a better-feeling place."

When it is your deliberate intention to feel good and you really care about how you feel, you will find more and more thoughts about more and more subjects that do feel good. And then you will be better prepared to interface with others who could be feeling good or bad. Because of your desire to feel good, you will have prepaved your experience with others with whom you will be interacting, and then it will be much easier for you to focus positively about their situation no matter what sort of mess they are in. But if you have not been tending to your own vibration and you have not been consistently holding yourself in good-feeling thoughts and vibrations, then you may be swept into their situation, and then you may very well feel discomfort.

We just want to emphasize that you are not feeling *their pain,* caused by their situation, but instead *you are feeling your own pain brought about by your own thinking.* There is great control in that knowledge, and, in fact, true freedom. *When you discover that you can control the way you feel because you can control the thoughts you think, then you are free to joyously move about your planet, but when you believe that the way you feel is dependent upon the behavior or situations of others—and you also understand that you have no control over those behaviors or situations—you do not feel free.* That, in fact, was the "pain" you were describing.

My Sympathy Is of No Value to Anyone?

Jerry said to us: "So, when I take my attention off of those who are in trouble, *I'll* feel good. But still, that doesn't help *them* feel better. In other words, I haven't solved the problem. I'm just avoiding the problem."

We replied: If you do not focus upon their problem, you can continue to feel good, but they will still have the problem. That is true, at first. But if you *do* focus upon their problem, you feel bad, they continue to feel bad—and they still have the problem. And if you continue to focus on their problem, you will have the problem, too, in time. However, if you do not focus upon their problem, but instead try to imagine their solution or a positive outcome, you feel good—and there is then the possibility of your influencing them to more positive thoughts and outcomes.

In simple terms: You are never of value to another (and you never offer a solution) when you are feeling negative emotion, because the presence of negative emotion within you means you are focused upon the lack of what is wanted, rather than what is wanted.

So if someone is having a bad experience and they come into your awareness with a powerful wind of negativity wrapped around them, if you have not already deliberately achieved your alignment with feeling good, you may be swept into their negativity; you may become part of their chain of pain, and you may very well pass your discomfort onto another, who will then pass it on to another, and so on.

But if you have been deliberately setting the tone of your day by putting your head on your pillow each night and saying, *Tonight, as I sleep, all attraction will stop, which means tomorrow I will have a new beginning; and tomorrow I will look for what I am wanting to see because I want to feel good—because feeling good is the most important thing!* as you awaken in the morning, you will be upon a fresh path bringing no negativity from the day before. And then, as you walk into a room and you see someone with pain coming toward you, as this person comes with his or her pain, you do not become part of it, but instead you provide a better example of happiness, for that which you *feel* is that which you radiate.

Now, it is not likely that just because you remain happy, others will immediately join you in your happiness. In fact, when there is a great disparity between the way you are feeling and the way others are feeling, you will have a difficult time relating to one another; but in time, if you maintain your positive vibrational stance, they will either join you in your positive place or they will vibrate right out of your experience. The only way unhappy people can stay in your experience is by your continuing attention to them.

If you and two other people were walking along a mountain ledge, and you were not watching where you were going and stumbled and fell over the edge and were hanging by a very flimsy vine, and one of your friends was very strong and sure-footed and the other was very clumsy and not focused, which one would you be glad was there? Looking for the positive aspects is the way you find your sure footing. It is *who-you-are* from an Inner Perspective. And as you consistently align with increasingly better-feeling thoughts, the powerful resources of the Universe become available to you.

To sympathize with others means to focus upon their situation until you feel as they feel, and since everyone has the potential of feeling wonderful or feeling awful—of succeeding at their desires or of failing at their desires—you have options about which aspects of them you sympathize with. We encourage you to sympathize with the best-feeling aspects of others that you can find; and, in doing so, you may influence them to an improved condition, also.

To Not Hurt When They Feel Hurt?

A man once asked, "How do you end a relationship without being hurt by the other person being hurt? If you decide that it's time to move on and the other person is not ready to move on, so he or she is very distraught, how can you keep your balance in a situation like that?"

We replied: When you attempt to guide your behavior by paying attention to how someone else feels about your behavior, you are powerless because you cannot control his or her perspective, and therefore you cannot achieve any consistent improvement in your own vibration or point of attraction or how you feel.

If you have decided to take the action of leaving a relationship before you have done the vibrational work of focusing upon *what* you want and *why* you want it, any action that you take can only bring you more of the same discomfort that you have been experiencing. And even once the relationship has ended and you are alone or beginning another relationship with another person, those old lingering negative vibrations will not allow a pleasant unfolding. Simply put, it is so much better to find your vibrational balance *before* you take the action of separation, or you may experience a rather long time of discomfort.

Let us examine the components of this situation and bring some clarity to your options: You have come to the conclusion as a result of being unhappy in this relationship for a while that it would be better to end it. In other words, you do believe that your chance of happiness is greater outside of the relationship than inside it. But when you announce that to your partner, your partner becomes even more unhappy. And now because your partner is more unhappy—you are more unhappy.

One option is to stay—to say, "Never mind. Don't be unhappy. I've changed my mind. I'll stay." But all that has happened is that you were both feeling unhappy; you made a decision to leave, which made your partner even more unhappy; and now you have pulled back from that decision, so your partner is now not quite as unhappy as before—but still neither of you are happy. So, nothing has changed except that things got a bit more intense for a while, but basically you are still unsatisfied and unhappy in this relationship.

Another option is to just leave. You could focus upon all of the things that have caused you to feel uncomfortable in the relationship and use those things as your justification for leaving. And while that negative focus upon negative things will give you the conviction to take the action of leaving, you will not really feel that much better. While you may feel some relief from the intensity of your unhappiness once you are on the outside of the relationship, you will continue to feel a need to justify your action of leaving, which will continue to hold you in an unpleasant state. So even though you have walked away from the things that were really bothering you, you will still feel bothered.

Really, there is nothing that you can *do* to prevent others from feeling bad, because they do not feel bad because of *your* behavior. There is no greater entrapment in relationships or in life than to attempt to keep others happy by observing *their* emotions and then trying to compensate with *your* actions.

The only way you can be happy is to decide to be happy. When you take upon yourself the responsibility of another's happiness, you are attempting the impossible and you are setting yourself up for a great deal of personal discord.

So now let us consider the options of *Pivoting* and *Positive Aspects:* Stay where you are for now, making no big change in your action or behavior. In other words, if you are living together, continue to do so. If you are spending time together, continue to do so. This option is a change in your *thought* process, not your *action* process. These processes are designed to help you to focus differently and to begin telling the story of your relationship, or of your life, in a better-feeling, more self-empowering way.

For example: *I've been thinking about leaving this relationship because I find that I'm not happy within it. But as I think about leaving, I realize that when I go, I'll take myself with me—and if I leave because I'm unhappy, I'll be taking that unhappy person with me. The reason that I want to leave is because I want to feel good. I wonder if it's possible to feel good without leaving. I wonder if there is anything about our relationship that I could focus upon that does feel good.*

I remember meeting this person and how that felt. I remember feeling drawn by this person and eager to move forward to see what more we might discover together. I liked the feeling of discovery. I liked our relationship as it began. I think that the more time we spent together, the more we both realized that we were not really a perfect match. I don't believe that there is any failure on either of our parts in that. Not being a perfect match doesn't mean that either of us is wrong. It only means that there are potentially better partners out there for each of us.

There are so many things about this person that I like and that anyone would easily appreciate: so smart, and interested in so many things; laughs easily and loves to have fun. . . . I'm glad that we've come together, and I believe our time together will prove to be of value to both of us.

So, our answer to your important question is this: You cannot control the pain that any other feels by modifying *your* behavior. You can, however, control your own pain by directing your thoughts until your pain subsides and is replaced by improved feelings. *As you give your attention to what you are wanting—you will always begin to feel good. As you give your attention to the lack of what you are wanting—you will always feel bad. And if you give your attention to the lack of what someone else is wanting—you will feel bad, also.*

You are so action oriented as physical Beings that you really think that you have to fix everything right now. Your partner did not get to this place all of a sudden. Your partner did not even get there only during your relationship. This has been a long path. Momentum has been gathering along the way. And so, do not expect that a conversation that you two are having in this moment is going to make all of the difference. See yourself as one who is planting a seed—a very strong, sure, powerful seed. You have planted it perfectly, and you have nurtured it for a time with your words so that long after you are gone, that seed will continue to blossom into that which it is to be.

There are many relationships that are not appropriate for you to continue, but we would never walk out of a relationship feeling angry, guilty, or defensive. Do the vibrational work, get to feeling good, and then leave. And then what comes next will not be a replay of what you just left.

I Am Not Responsible for Others' Creations

You must not accept the responsibility for what others are doing in their own life experience. See them as emerging from the lack, and know that it is going to be better for them later—and then *you* will begin to feel better. You may even inspire them, in their sleep state, to an improved direction. When you think about them, see them as happy. Do not regurgitate, in your mind, the sad conversations you have had or the parting. Envision them as getting on with their life just as you are getting on with yours. *Trust that they have the Guidance within them to find their own way.*

What trips most of you up so often in your wanting to help others is that you believe, *They need my help because they cannot help themselves,* but that belief is detrimental to them because deep down inside, they know that they *can* do it, and that they are *wanting* to do it.

Begin to say things to your partner such as: "You are such a fantastic person. And while we haven't connected on as many levels as I would like, I know that there is a perfect partner waiting for you, and I'm releasing you to that wonderful opportunity. Look for it! I don't want to keep you caged here, captive to something that neither one of us wants. I want to free us both to that which we both are wanting. I'm not telling you good-bye forever; I'm saying, 'Let this relationship have a new understanding between us, one that is inspired from passionate, positive desire, not one that is whipped into place because we are afraid of the possible consequences.'"

And then say to the person, "When I think of you, I will always know that while you are sad now, you are going to be happy later. I'm going to choose to see you as happy, because that's the way I like you best, and that's what you prefer, too."

This may sound tough or cold. But nothing else makes sense.

Listen for Guidance, or Reach for Good Feelings?

You have the ability to pivot under any and all conditions. It does not matter how negative something seems—you have the ability to give your attention to the positive aspects of it. The only things that get in your way are some old habits, or maybe some strong influences from others.

Most people are habitual in nature, and your patterns are so well entrenched that at times the fastest path to the joy you seek is for you to take your pivot as you sleep—and then awaken in the new day already in the direction of that which you are wanting. By reaching for good-feeling thoughts before you go to sleep and then experiencing the benefit of the quiet mind that occurs while you sleep—and then upon awakening, immediately turning to good-feeling thoughts—you can accomplish the ultimate *Pivoting* experience. A few days of following that pattern will provide a big change in your habit of thought and your point of attraction, and you will discover improvement in virtually every aspect of your life.

What If I Played the *What-If?* Game?

As we encourage that you do your best to find positive aspects upon whatever subject is before you, there are often those who would ask: "But what about the man who's just lost his job and has a wife and five children, his rent is due in two days, and he doesn't have the money to pay it? Or, what about the woman who has the gestapo army at her door, about to take her to be killed in a gas chamber? How could those people pivot?"

And to those extreme questions, we often reply: It is as if you have just jumped out of an airplane at an altitude of 20,000 feet and you have no parachute, and you ask, "So *now* what do I do?" You are usually not faced with such extreme circumstances from which it seems there is no possible, comfortable escape. However, these extreme situations, with all of the drama and trauma that they bring, also bring a power that, with the right focus, can provide resolutions that someone watching from the outside would find astonishing or even miraculous.

In other words, there is no situation from which you cannot find a positive resolution, but you have to be able to focus powerfully in order to accomplish such a solution. And most people who are in those kinds of situations are not adept at that kind of focus—which is why they are experiencing the negative situation to begin with.

When you are involved in extreme situations, a power comes forth from within, and so the intensity of your desire will put you upon a plateau where, if you can just get focused, you can have your greater elevation. In other words, those who are very sick are in a better position to be even more *well* than most others, because their *desire* for wellness is amplified. But unless they are able to pivot (to turn their attention to their desire for wellness and away from their concern about illness), they cannot become well.

We would encourage you to play the *What-If?* game, looking for positive aspects. In other words, rather than looking into your society for examples of disempowered people having no control over the circumstances of their lives, tell a story that gives you a feeling of empowerment. Instead of telling the story of powerless victims and thereby amplifying your own feeling of also being a victim, tell a different story.

For example: *What if* this woman, before the gestapo army came pounding on her door, had recognized the rumblings of the looming Holocaust that were in the community weeks before? *What if* she had left the community when many of the others had left? *What if* she had not been afraid of the unknown? *What if* she had not held to the familiar? *What if* she had made the decision to start a new life in a new country with her sister and her aunt and uncle two weeks ago so that she was not at home when the gestapo came calling?

When you play the *What-If?* game, look for things you *do want* to see. Look for things that make you feel better.

There is never a situation in which there is not a way out. In fact, there are hundreds and thousands of practical choices along the way— but, out of habit, most people continue to choose the "lack" perspective in situations until they eventually find themselves in an unwanted place where it seems that there are no more choices.

As you hold to your intention to look for evidence of Well-Being and thriving and success and happiness, you will tune yourself to the vibrations of *those* things—and so those kinds of good-feeling experiences will dominate your life. *Today, no matter where I am going, no matter what I am doing, it is my dominant intent to look for what I am wanting to see.*

As you make the decision that you are not a mere observer of your world, but a deliberate and positive contributor *to* your world, you will find great pleasure in your involvement with what is going on upon your planet. When you witness things that you do not want to happen in your world, in your nation, in your neighborhood, in your family, or in your personal body, and you remember that you have the power to tell a different story—and you also know that there is enormous power in telling a different story—you will then step back into the exuberant knowledge that you held when you made the decision to come forth to participate on this planet to begin with.

You cannot be in a place other than where you are right now, but you do have the power to begin to express your perspective about where you are in increasingly better ways. And as you do that consciously and deliberately, you will see the evidence of the power of your focus on every subject to which you turn your attention.

As you make the decision that you want to feel good and you consciously look for positive aspects within the subjects that you are involved in every day, and as you deliberately identify and focus upon what you *do* want regarding these subjects, you will set yourself upon a path of Eternal unfolding satisfaction and joy.

These processes are simple to understand and to apply, but do not let their simplicity cause you to underestimate their power. Consistently apply them and show yourself the leverage of the power of aligned thought. Discover the power of the Energy that creates worlds—the power that you have always had ready access to but which you now understand how to apply—and focus it toward your own personal creations.

PART II

Attracting
Money
and Manifesting
Abundance

(**Editor's Note:** In the sections where there is a back-and-forth dialogue between Jerry and Abraham, the speaker's name is repeated at the beginning of each section for clarity.)

Attracting Money and Manifesting Abundance

While money is not absolutely essential to your experience, to most people *money* and *freedom* are synonymous. And since an intense awareness of your right to be free is at the very core of that which you are, it follows, therefore, that your relationship with money is one of the most important subjects of your life experience. And so, it is no wonder you have such strong feelings about the subject of money.

Although some people have discovered the freedom of allowing large amounts of money to flow through their experiences, it is more often the case that because you are experiencing far less money than you need or desire, most of you are not feeling free. It is our intention, here, to clearly explain why this financial disparity exists so that you can begin to allow the abundance that you want and deserve into your experience. For, as you read these words and as you begin to resonate with these *Law*-based truths, you will align your desire with the abundance of your world, and the evidence of your newfound alignment will soon become apparent to you and to others who observe you.

Whether you are one who has been working to achieve financial abundance for many years or you are a youngster just starting down that path, the journey to financial Well-Being does not have to be a long one from where you are. And it does not require large amounts of time or physical effort, for we are going to explain to you in simple and easy-to-understand terms how to utilize the leverage of Energy that is available to you. We want to show you the absolute correlation between the thoughts you have been thinking about money, the way you feel when you think those thoughts—and the money that flows into your experience. When you are able to consciously make that correlation, and you decide to deliberately direct your thoughts accordingly, you will access the power of the Universe and you will then see how time and physical effort are rather irrelevant to your financial success.

So we begin with the simple premise of your Universe and of your world: *You get what you think about.* Often people say to us, "That can't be true, because I have wanted and thought about more money for as long as I can remember, but I continue to struggle with not enough money." And what we then tell them is the most important thing for you to understand if you want to improve your financial situation: *The subject of money is really two subjects: (1) money, plenty of money, the feeling of freedom and ease that plenty of money can provide; and (2) absence of money, not nearly enough money, the feeling of fear and disappointment that the thought of absence of money induces.*

Often people assume that because they are speaking the words "I want more money," they are speaking positively about money. But when you are speaking of money (or anything) and you are feeling fear or discomfort as you speak, you are not speaking of the subject of money, but instead you are speaking of the subject of not enough money. And the difference is very important, because the first statement brings money and the second holds it away.

It is of value for you to become aware of how you are really *thinking* and, more important, *feeling* about money. If you are thinking or saying things like: "Oh, that is a very beautiful thing—but I cannot afford it," you are not in a vibrational position to allow in the abundance you desire. The feeling of disappointment that is present as you acknowledge that you cannot afford it is your indicator that the balance of your thought is pointed more toward the lack of your desire than toward the desire itself. *The negative emotion that you feel as you acknowledge that you cannot afford something that you want is one way of understanding the balance of your thoughts, and the amount of abundance that you are actually experiencing is another way of knowing.*

Many people continue to perpetuate the experience of "not enough" in their lives simply because they do not think beyond the reality of what they are actually experiencing. In other words, if they are experiencing the shortage of money and are aware of it and speak of it often, they hold themselves in that chronic position. And so, many people protest when we explain to them the power of telling the story of their finances as they want it to be rather than as it is, because they believe that they should be factual about what is happening.

But we want you to understand that if you continue to look at *what-is* and speak of *what-is*, you will not find the improvement that you desire. You may see a parade of changing faces and places, but your life experience will essentially show no improvement. If you want to effect substantial change in your life experience, you have to offer substantially different vibrations, which means you must think thoughts that *feel* different as you think them.

Lackful Action Doesn't Pay Off

Jerry: Many years ago I owned a motel near El Paso, Texas, and H. L. Hunt, who at that time was one of the wealthiest men in the United States (one of the multibillionaires), called me. He had purchased Ojo Caliente, a small resort on the Rio Grande that was financially failing, and he had heard that I might have some useful information to help him turn it around. As we were visiting in my little coffee shop, I had a difficult time focusing on our conversation because I just couldn't understand why a man that wealthy would still be discontent and looking for a way of making more money. I wondered why he didn't just sell the place—at whatever price—and go on about his life enjoying the money he had already accumulated.

I have another friend who's in the multibillionaire class. We were in Rio de Janeiro, Brazil, walking on the beach, and he was talking about some business problems he was having, and it really struck me that that man—so wealthy—would have *any* kind of troubles. But what I've learned from you, Abraham (and I've learned a lot from you), is that our true success in life is not about how much money we have or about the having of things. Right?

First, I'll Find My Vibrational Balance

Abraham: The things that you *have* and the things that you *do* are all meant to enhance your state of *being*. In other words, it's all about how you feel, and how you feel is all about coming into alignment with *who-you-really-are*. When you tend to your alignment first, then the things you gather and the actions you perform only enhance your good-feeling state of being . . . but if you do not find that vibrational balance first and attempt to make yourself feel better by bringing more things into your experience or participating in more activities in order to try to make yourself feel better, you just get further out of balance.

We are not guiding you away from accumulating things or from taking action, because all of that is an essential part of your physical experience. In other words, you intended the wonderful experience of exploring the details of your physical world in order to help you to personally determine your own joyous growth and expansion, but when you try to move forward from an imbalanced footing, it is always uncomfortable. *If you will begin by identifying how you want to feel, or be, and let your inspiration to accumulate or to do come from that centered place, then not only will you maintain your balance, but you will now enjoy the things you gather and the things that you do.*

Most people do most of their wanting from a place of lack. They want things, in many cases, simply because they do not have them, so the having of them does not really satisfy anything deep within them because there is always something else that they do not have. And so, it becomes a never-ending struggle to try to bring one more thing (one more thing that still will not be satisfying) into their experience: *Because I don't have this, I want it.* And they really think that getting it will fill the void. But that defies *Law*.

Any action that is taken from a place of lack is always counterproductive, and it always leads to more of a feeling of lack. The void that these people are feeling cannot be filled with things or satisfied with action because the feeling of void is about the vibrational discord between their desires and their chronic habits of thought.

Offering better-feeling thoughts, telling a different story, looking for positive aspects, *Pivoting* to the subject of what you really *do* want, looking for positive *what-ifs*—that is how you fill that void. And when you do, a most interesting thing will occur in your experience: The things you have wanted will begin to flood into your experience. But these things you have been wanting will flood in not to fill your void, because that void no longer exists—they flow in *because* your void no longer exists.

Certainly, you will gather many magnificent things into your experience. *Our message is not for you to stop <u>wanting, having,</u> or <u>doing.</u> Our message is for you to <u>want</u> and <u>accumulate</u> and <u>do</u> from your place of feeling good.*

Neither Money Nor Poverty Makes Joy

Jerry: Abraham, there's a saying that money doesn't make for happiness. On the other hand, I've noticed that poverty doesn't make for happiness either, but still it's obvious that money isn't the *path* to happiness. So, if the *idea* of achieving something does bring us happiness, does that mean the *achievement* is an appropriate goal for us to set? And how does a person maintain his or her feeling of happiness when reaching one's goal is taking a lot of time and energy? It often seems that there is a sort of uphill climb to reach the goal and then a short plateau of rest, but then an almost immediate tedious climb to achieve the next goal.

How does a person keep all of the climbing toward their goals joyous so there's not that struggle, struggle, struggle, and then: "Wow, I've made it!" but then struggle, struggle, struggle—"Oh, here I've made it again"?

Abraham: You are right! Money is not the path to happiness, and as you have observed, poverty certainly is not the path to happiness either.

It is so important to remember that when you offer any action for the purpose of achieving happiness, you are truly going about it in a backward way. Instead, use your ability to focus your thoughts and words toward things that cause you to feel better and better; and once you have deliberately achieved a state of happiness, not only will wonderful actions be *inspired,* but wonderful results must follow.

Most people give the majority of their attention to whatever is happening in their experience right now—which means if the results please them, they feel good, but if the results do not please them, they feel bad. But that is really going about life the hard way. If you only have the ability to see *what-is,* then things cannot improve. You must find a way to look optimistically forward in order to achieve any improvement in your experience.

When you learn how to deliberately focus your thoughts toward good-feeling things, it is not difficult to find happiness and main-tain it even before your goal has been accomplished. The feeling of struggle you were describing happens because of the continual comparison of where you are right now in relationship to the goal you are reaching for. When you constantly take score, noticing the distance that still needs to be traveled, you amplify the distance, the task, and the effort; and that is why it feels like such an uphill struggle.

When you care about how you feel, and so choose thoughts on the basis of how they feel, you then develop patterns of thought that are more forward looking. And as the *Law of Attraction* then responds to those better-feeling thoughts, you get more pleasing results. *Struggle, struggle, struggle never leads to a happy ending. It defies Law. "When I get there, then I'll be happy" is not a productive mind-set because unless you are happy, you cannot get there. When you decide to first be happy—then you will get there.*

I Am Here as a Joyful Creator

Abraham: You are here not as accumulators or regurgitators. You are here as *creators.* When you are looking toward an ending place, you exaggerate the feeling of lack between where you are now and that ending place—and that habit of thought can not only slow the progress of your creation, but can hold it apart from you indefinitely. *You are the attractor of your experience. As you look for positive aspects and make an effort to find good-feeling thoughts, you will hold yourself in a place of positive attraction and what you want will come faster.*

The sculptor of a work of art does not derive his greatest satisfaction from the finished piece. It is the process of creation (the sculpting of the piece) that gives him pleasure. That is the way we would like you to view your physical experience of creating: *continual, joyful becoming.* As you focus your attention upon things that feel good and achieve a consistently joyful state of being, you will then be in the position of attracting more of whatever you want.

Sometimes people complain that it seems unfair that they have to become happy before things that bring more happiness can then come to them. They believe that when they are unhappy, they "need" the happy events to come, but when they are already happy, then the happy events are unnecessary—but that would defy the *Law of Attraction. You have to find a way of feeling the <u>essence</u> of what you desire before the <u>details</u> of that desire can come to you. In other words, you have to begin to feel more prosperous before more prosperity can come.*

Often people tell us that they want more money, and when we ask them what their balance of thought is about money, they proclaim that they have a very positive attitude about money. But as we probe a bit deeper, asking them how they feel when they sit to pay their bills, they often then realize that while they may have been attempting to sound positive about the subject, they have actually been feeling a great deal of worry or even fear around the subject of money. In other words, often without realizing it, the majority of their thoughts about money have been on the *not-enough* side of the subject rather than on the *abundant* side of the subject.

The Power of Vibrationally Spending Vibrational Money

Abraham: Here is a process that can quickly help you shift the balance of your thoughts regarding money to a place where you can begin to let more money flow easily into your experience: Put $100 in your pocket and keep it with you at all times. As you move through your day, deliberately notice how many things you could exchange this money for: "I could purchase that. I could do that."

Someone replied to us that $100 really does not buy that much in today's economy, but we explained that if you mentally spend that $100 one thousand times today, you have vibrationally spent $100,000. That sort of positive focus will dramatically change your vibrational balance about money. This vibrational spending process will cause you to feel differently about money; and when that happens, your point of attraction will shift—and more money must flow into your experience. *It is _Law._*

Someone said to us, "Abraham, I didn't have the $100, but I put an IOU in my pocket." And we said, that is defeating the process, because you are walking around with a *feeling* of debt in your pocket, which is exactly the opposite of what you want to do. You want to *feel* your prosperity. And so, even if it is only $20 or $50, or if it is $1,000 or $10,000, that you have in your pocket, *utilize it effectively to help you notice how good things are—now.* Because in your acknowledgment of your prosperous *now*—your prosperity must become more.

Needing Money Won't Attract It

Jerry: Abraham, one of my greatest disappointments as I have worked to help people find greater financial success is that those who *needed* the money the *most* had the *least* success with what I was teaching them, while those who *needed* it the *least* had the *most* success with it. That always seemed backward to me: It seemed like those who needed it more would try harder, and eventually they should succeed.

Abraham: Anyone who is in a place of lack—no matter how much action they offer—attracts more lack. In other words, the powerful *feeling* outweighs any *action* that they offer. *Any action that is offered from a place of lack is always counterproductive.* Those who were not feeling need were not in a place of lack, and so their action was productive. Your experience was in absolute harmony with the *Law of Attraction*—as is every experience. There is not a shred of evidence anywhere in the Universe that is to the contrary of this that we are speaking of.

Jerry: Also, what I noticed was that by and large, those who didn't achieve much success, or weren't very interested in even hearing about achieving success, were people who had been taught that to want money was evil or immoral, and that the best thing for them to do was to remain as they were even though they were unfulfilled.

Abraham: The reason that many reach a place where they say that they do not have desire is because they have wanted and wanted and wanted, but because they have not understood that every subject is two subjects, they have given more of their attention to the lack of what they have wanted than to what they wanted. And so, they continued to attract the lack of what they want. And then, eventually, they were just worn down by it. As a person begins to associate wanting with not having, so much so that to want is an unpleasant experience, then he or she says, "I no longer want, because every time I want something, I get myself in this place of discomfort, and so it is easier for me not to want in the first place."

What If a "Poor" One Doesn't Feel Poor?

Jerry: If others who are noticing you and comparing you to themselves come to the conclusion that you are poor but *you* don't *feel* poor, then you wouldn't be in a state of lack—and so you would be able to move quickly toward more abundance in that case, right?

Abraham: That is correct. Others' assessment of you has no bearing on your point of attraction unless you are bothered by their assessment. Comparing your experience to the experiences of others can amplify a feeling of lack within you if you come to the conclusion that they have succeeded more greatly than you have, and you then activate within yourself a feeling of being "less than." Also, noticing a lack of prosperity in the experiences of others does not put you in a place of attracting greater prosperity for yourself, because you will be getting what you think about.

What you draw to you—or keep from you—has nothing to do with what anyone else is doing. *An improved feeling of prosperity, even if your current reality does not justify the feeling, will always bring more prosperity to you. Paying attention to the way you feel about money is a much more productive activity than noticing how others are doing.*

Allowing more money to flow into your experience requires far less than most people understand. All that is required is that you achieve a vibrational balance in your own thoughts. If you want more money but doubt you can achieve it—you are not in balance. If you want more money but you believe there is something wrong in having money—you are not in balance. If you want more money and you are angry at those who have more money—you are not in balance. When you are feeling those emotions of inadequacy, insecurity, jealousy, injustice, anger, and so on, your *Emotional Guidance System* is letting you know that you are out of alignment with your own desire.

Most people make no effort in coming into personal alignment with the subject of money. Instead, they spend years, even lifetimes, pointing out perceived injustices, attempting to define the rightness or wrongness of the subject, and even trying to put laws in place to orchestrate the flow of money in the civilization, when a rather small effort—in comparison with the impossible attempt at controlling those outside circumstances—would yield them an enormous return.

Nothing is more important than that you feel good, for when you feel good, you are in harmony with your greater intent. Many believe that hard work and struggle are not only a requirement to achieve success, but that working hard and struggling long is a more honorable way of living life. Those hard times of struggle certainly do ... in the defining of what you desire, but until you release the feeling of struggle, what you desire cannot come into your experience.

Often people feel as if they need to prove their worthiness, and that once that is accomplished, then and only then will rewards be given—but we want you to know that you are already worthy, and that proving yourselves worthy is not only not possible, but unnecessary. What *is* necessary for you to receive the rewards or benefits that you seek is alignment with the essence of those benefits. You have to first bring yourself into vibrational alignment with the experiences you wish to live.

We recognize that words do not teach and that our knowledge regarding the *Laws of the Universe* and of your value do not necessarily mean that now that you have read our words, you now know your value. However, as you consider the premises that we are laying out for you here, and as you begin the application of the processes that we are suggesting here, it is our knowing that the Universe's response to your improved vibration will give you the evidence of the existence of these *Laws.*

It will not be long and it will not require much deliberate application of what you are reading here before you will be convinced of your own value and of your ability to create whatever you desire. The primary reason that people do not believe in their own value is because they often have not found a way to get what they want, and so they incorrectly assume that someone outside of them does not approve and is somehow withholding the reward. That is never true. You are the creator of your experience.

Make statements such as: *I want to be the best that I can be. I want to do and have and live in a way that is in harmony with my idea of the greatest goodness. I want to harmonize physically here in this body with that which I believe to be the best, or the good way, of life.* If you will make those statements, and then do not take action unless you feel good, you will always be moving upon the path in harmony with your idea of that which is good.

What Is My "Financial Abundance" Story?

Abraham: A belief in lack is the reason that more people are not allowing themselves the financial abundance they desire. When you believe that there is a finite pile of abundance and that there is not enough to go around—and so you feel injustice when someone has more than others, believing that because they have it, others are deprived of having it—you are holding yourself apart from abundance. It is not another's achievement of success that is responsible for your lack of achievement, but rather it is your negative comparison and your attention to the lack of your own desire. When you feel the negative emotion that you feel as you accuse others of injustice or of squandering wealth or hoarding—or when you simply believe that there is not enough to go around— you hold yourself in the position of denying your own improved condition.

What anyone else has or does not have has nothing to do with you. The only thing that affects your experience is the way you utilize the Non-Physical Energy with your thought. Your abundance or lack of it in your experience has nothing to do with what anybody else is doing or having. It has only to do with your perspective. It has only to do with your offering of thought. If you want your fortunes to shift, you have to begin telling a different story.

Many people criticize those who are living well, who accumulate land and money and things; and that criticism is symptomatic of their own lackful habit of thought. They want to feel better and often believe that if they can make that which they are unable to achieve "wrong," then they will feel better—but they never do feel better, because their attention to lack perpetuates lack everywhere they look. They would not feel uncomfortable in seeing someone else's achievement if that desire for achievement were not present within themselves as well. And that criticism that they often keep alive within themselves only serves to hold them in vibrational discord with what they want.

In other words, if someone called you on the telephone and said to you, "Hello, you don't know me, but I'm calling to tell you that I will never call you again," you would not feel negative emotion about the caller's absence from your life, because his or her presence was not something that you desired to begin with. But if someone you care about were to make that announcement to you, you would feel strong negative emotion, because your desire and your belief would then be at odds.

When you feel negative emotion about anything, it always means that you have a desire that has been born from your personal life experience that you are, right now, opposing with other thoughts. *Vibrational discord is always the reason for negative emotion. And negative emotion is always guidance to help you redirect your thoughts to find vibrational alignment with who-you-really-are and with your current desires.*

What If the Poor Criticize the Rich?

Jerry: When I was a kid, I associated with poor people primarily, and we used to make fun of those who were wealthy—we criticized those who drove luxury cars, for instance. And so, as an adult, when it came time that I would like to have owned a Cadillac, I couldn't bring myself to drive one because I felt that people would make fun of me as I had made fun of the others. So I drove a Mercedes because years ago people kind of thought that they were "economy" cars.

The only way I could bring myself to drive a Cadillac, which I finally did, was to bridge my thoughts by saying, *Well, by buying this car, I put all those people to work who put this car together. I created jobs for all the people who supplied the parts and the materials—the leather, the metal, the glass—and the craftsmen, and so on. . . .* And in that justification, then I was able to buy the car. So somehow I discovered a process of bridging my thoughts that helped me allow that symbol of success into my experience.

Abraham: Your process of bridging thoughts is an effective one. When you want to feel good and you gradually find increasingly better-feeling thoughts, you are bringing yourself into alignment with your desire and you are releasing the resistance that is preventing your improved conditions. *Focusing on opposing opinions of others is never productive because it always causes discord within you, which also prevents your improved condition. There will always be others who disagree with you, and your attention to them will always cause you to <u>vibrationally</u> disagree with your own desires. Listen to your own <u>Guidance System</u>—by paying attention to how you are feeling—in order to determine the appropriateness of your desires and behaviors.*

There will always be someone, no matter which side of any subject you choose, who does not harmonize with you. And that is why we speak so firmly, and want so much for you to understand, that your greatest endeavor is to find harmony with *who-you-really-are.* If you would trust in yourself—if you could believe that through all that you have lived you have come to a place of very strong knowing, and that you can trust the way you feel as your personal form of Guidance about the appropriateness or inappropriateness of what you are contemplating doing—then you would utilize your *Guidance System* in the way that it was really intended.

What If Our Money Loses Value?

Jerry: Abraham, in the past our money was primarily coins—metal that had a value in and of itself: Like the $20 gold piece, the gold itself was worth $20; and the silver in the silver dollar had value. And so, it seemed simple to understand the value of the coin. But now our money in and of itself has no actual value; the paper and coins are essentially valueless.

I've always appreciated the convenience of money as a way of exchanging goods and talents rather than trading a chicken for a container of milk or for a basket of potatoes. But now our money is being artificially devalued, and it's becoming increasingly difficult to really understand the value of a dollar. In other words, it reminds me of my own searching for my own value: "How much is my talent worth? How much should I ask for in exchange for the time and energy that I put forth?" But now I'm learning from you that we don't have to consider our value in that way. We have only to consider what it is that we want and then allow it in.

I'm aware that many people are feeling insecure about their financial future because they feel they don't have control over what may happen to the value of the dollar—because it's typically a handful of people who seem to control or manipulate that. Many worry that there's going to be more inflation, or even another depression. I'd like people to understand what you've been teaching us about the *Law of Attraction* so that they won't be concerned with things that are outside of their control, like the value of the dollar.

Abraham: You have hit upon something very essential here regarding the subject of money because, you are right, many of you are recognizing that the dollars today just are not worth what they were at one time. But that is another position of lack you very often stand firmly upon that keeps you from attracting the abundance that is yours.

We would like you to understand that the dollar and its assigned value is really not as important to your experience as you are believing, and that if you could put your attention upon what you are wanting, in terms of *being* and then *having* and then *doing,* that all of the money—or other means for bringing about what you want—could then flow easily, and much more effortlessly, into your experience.

We keep coming back to the same terminology: *From your place of lack, you cannot attract its opposite. And so, it really is a matter of adjusting your thinking so that your thinking harmonizes with that which feels good within you.*

Every thought that you think vibrates, and it is by virtue of having that vibrating thought that you attract. When you think a thought of lack, that thought is vibrating at a place that is so alien to that which your *Inner Being* knows to be that your *Inner Being* cannot resonate with you at all—and the resultant feeling within you is one of negative emotion. When you think a thought of upliftment or abundance or Well-Being, those thoughts do harmonize with that which your *Inner Being* knows to be. And under those conditions, you are filled with a feeling of positive emotion.

You may trust the way that you feel as the indicator as to which side of this subject (that is really two subjects) you are on. *Whether*

it is the subject of money or lack of it, or health or lack of it, or a rela-
tionship or the lack of one—always, when you feel good, you are in the
place of attracting that which you are wanting.

To Reverse a Downward Spiral?

Jerry: When I would see people having financial problems, I used to worry about them. I would watch as they spiraled down, down, down, until they would finally come crashing down in bankruptcy. But then in a very short time, they would have another new boat, a new luxury car, and another beautiful home. In other words, no one I watched seemed to stay down. But why couldn't they stop the downward spiral somewhere earlier along the way and start back upward sooner? Why did so many of them have to go all the way to the bottom before they could start back up again?

Abraham: The reason for any downward spiral is attention to lack. In their fear that they might lose something, or in their attention to things that they were losing, they were focused upon the lack of what they wanted; and as long as that was their point of attention, only more loss was possible. As they felt guarded or defensive, or as they began to justify or rationalize or blame, they were on the lack side of the equation and only more lack could be their experience.

But once they hit bottom and were no longer in a place of guardedness because there was nothing else to lose, their attention shifted, and so their vibration shifted—and so their point of attraction shifted. Hitting what they believed to be the bottom caused them to begin to look up. You could say that it forced them to begin telling a different story.

Your life experience has caused you to ask for many wonderful things that are making their way into your experience, but your worry or doubt or fear or resentment or blame or jealousy (or any number of negative emotions) would indicate that the predominant thoughts you were thinking were holding those things away. It would be as if you had drawn them right outside your door, but your door was closed. As you begin to tell a different story of the things you could buy with a $100 bill, as you relax and focus more upon the positive aspects of your life, as you more deliberately choose the better-feeling end of the vibrational stick—that door will open and you will be flooded with manifestations of those wanted things and experiences and relationships.

A War Against War Is War

Abraham: Recognizing that you are the creator of your own life experience and learning to deliberately do so by directing your thoughts is an adjustment for most people, because most have long believed that you *make* things happen through *action.* Not only have you erroneously believed that action is what makes things happen, but you have also believed that if you apply pressure to unwanted things, they will go away. That is why you have a "war against poverty" and a "war against drugs" and a "war against AIDS" and a "war against terrorism."

And although you may believe that pushing against these unwanted things will cause them to leave your experience, that is not how the *Laws of the Universe* work, and that is not the proof of your experience, for all of those wars are getting bigger. *Attention to the lack of what is wanted causes it to increase and come closer to you, just as focusing upon what is wanted causes it to increase and come closer to you.*

When you relax into your natural Well-Being, when you make statements such as: "I seek abundance, and I trust the *Laws of the Universe*—I have identified the things that I want, and now I am going to relax and allow them into my experience," more of what you desire will come. If your financial situation feels like a struggle, you are pushing your financial Well-Being farther away, but when you begin to feel ease regarding your financial situation, you are then allowing more abundance to flow into your experience. It really is as simple as that.

And so, when you see others excelling in their attraction of money and you feel negative emotion about it, that is your signal that your current thought is not allowing the abundance that you desire into your experience. *When you find yourself critical of the way anyone has attracted or is using money, you are pushing money away from yourself. But when you realize that what others do with money has nothing to do with you, and that your primary work is to think and speak and do what feels good to you, then you will be in alignment not only about the subject of money, but about every important subject in your physical experience.*

Can We Succeed Without Talent?

Jerry: What bearing does talent or skill or ability have on bringing abundance or money into our lives?

Abraham: Very little. Those are all *action* aspects for the most part, and your *action* is responsible for but a minuscule part of what comes to you. Your *thoughts* and *words* (words are *thoughts* articulated) are the reason your life unfolds as it does.

Jerry: So then would you say that people with no salable skill or talent could still receive all the financial abundance they want in their lives?

Abraham: Absolutely, unless in comparing themselves to others (and concluding that they have no salable skill or talent), they feel diminished and therefore defeat their own experience with their own negative expectation.

The most valuable skill that you could ever develop is the skill of directing your thoughts toward what you want—to be adept at quickly evaluating all situations and then quickly coming to the conclusion of what you most want—and then giving your undivided attention to that. There is a tremendous skill in directing your own thoughts that will yield results that cannot be compared with results that mere action can provide.

Can We Get Something Without Giving?

Jerry: So, how can people get past the belief that they must *give* a dollar's worth of something in order to *get* a dollar's worth of something?

Abraham: Your knowledge in all things comes only through life experience, but your life experience comes as a result of the thoughts that you are thinking. So even though you may have wanted something for a very long time, if your thoughts have been upon the absence of it, then it could not come to you. And so, from your personal experience, you come to the conclusion that it *is not* possible, or that it *is* a struggle. In other words, you come to many valid conclusions about things being hard when you have led a difficult life.

It is our desire to help you understand what is really at the heart of that self-created struggle. We want to help you begin from a different premise and understand the *Laws* at the basis of all things. A new understanding of the *Laws of the Universe* and a willingness to begin telling a different story will give you different results, and those different results will then give you different beliefs or knowledge.

You are the one, and the only one, who can evaluate your effectiveness. No one else has the ability to discern where you stand relative to where you are wanting to be, and nobody else can decide where you should be—only you.

They Want to Win the Lottery Fortune

Jerry: Many people are hoping for some major financial windfall to come to them to free them from debt or to release them from working at something they don't want to work at in order to receive money. The thing I hear them say most often is that they want to win the lottery, where they'll get their abundance in exchange for someone else losing theirs.

Abraham: If their *expectation* were in a place that would allow it, then that could be a way for money to come to them. But most know the odds against that, and so their *expectation* for winning the lottery is not in a powerful place either.

Jerry: So, how does *hoping to win* relate to *expecting to win?*

Abraham: Just as *hoping* is more productive than *doubting—expecting* is much more productive than *hoping.*

Jerry: Then how could people begin to expect something that their life experience hasn't yet shown them? How can you expect something that you haven't experienced?

Abraham: You do not have to *have* money to *attract* money, but you cannot *feel poor* and attract money. The key is, you have to find ways of improving the way you feel from right where you stand before things can begin to change: *By softening your attention to the things that are going wrong, and by beginning to tell stories that lean more in the direction of what you want instead of in the direction of what you have got, your vibration will shift, your point of attraction will shift, and you will get different results. And in a short time, because of the different results you are then getting, you will then have beliefs or knowledge of abundance that will easily perpetuate more of the same. People often say, "The rich get richer, and the poor get poorer," and that is why.*

Look for reasons to feel good. Identify what you want—and hold your thoughts in a place that feels good.

Living Abundantly Is Not "Magic"

Abraham: As we explain, from our perspective, the abundant nature of your Universe and the potential for abundance that is always available to you, we understand that our knowledge does not become your knowledge only because you have read our words. If we were to ask you to trust what we say or to "just try" to understand, you cannot just adopt our understanding as your own—for it is only your own life experience that brings knowledge to you.

The beliefs that you hold as a result of your own experience are very strong, and we understand that you cannot release them immediately and replace them with others, even though we know there are many more productive beliefs that you could foster. But there is something that you can begin today that will make a profound difference in the way your life unfolds that does not require an immediate releasing of the beliefs that you currently hold: *Start telling a more positive, better-feeling story about your life and the things that are important to you.*

Do not write your story like a factual documentary, weighing all the pros and cons of your experience, but instead tell the uplifting, fanciful, magical story of the wonder of your own life and watch what happens. It will feel like magic as your life begins to transform right before yours eyes, but it is not by magic. It is by the power of the *Laws of the Universe* and your deliberate alignment with those *Laws.*

Trading Freedom for Money?

Jerry: Well, I know we titled this book *Money, and the Law of Attraction,* but it's really more about attracting *abundance* in all areas of our lives. Since my childhood, we (in the U.S.) have been fighting strongly against crime. And there's much more crime now than when I was a kid. I read recently that our nation has a higher percentage of its population in prisons than any other country in the "free" world.

We've been fighting against illness, and yet there are more hospitals and more sick people than ever before—there's so much more physical suffering in this nation percentage-wise now than I've ever seen.

We've been pushing against warfare in our search for world peace, and yet it seems like such a short time ago that everyone was raving, "Isn't it wonderful [as the Berlin wall came down] that we're finally in peace?" But we hardly took four breaths until we were back in another series of wars, and now *we're* even putting more walls up around *this* nation.

Also, I hear of so much concern about child abuse and the mistreating of other people, and yet the more I hear of our pushing against child abuse, the more child abuse I hear of.

It seems like everything we're trying to do to stop what we don't want isn't working for us. But the area where this nation seems to continue to go in a more positive direction is that of *abundance*. We have so much food and money that we're able to give the world over from our excess abundance, and I see many more material things in the hands of more people in this country than during my early years, so there have been some major positive changes there.

But so many people, in their quest for more financial abundance, seem to be losing quite a bit of their personal freedom as a trade-off for the money. It seems like there are those who seem to have a lot of free time, but they have so little money that they don't enjoy their time. And then there are those with more money, but little time to enjoy the money. But it's rare that I meet someone who has both an abundant flow of money combined with the time to really enjoy it. Abraham, would you please comment on your perspective of my perceptions?

Abraham: Whether you are focused upon the lack of money or the lack of time, you are still focused upon the lack of something you want and therefore holding yourself in resistance to the things you really want. Whether your negative emotion is because of your feeling of shortage of time or whether it is because of your feeling of shortage of money, you are still feeling negative emotion and you are still in a state of resistance, and therefore you are holding away what you really want.

As you feel that you do not have enough time to do all of the things you need or want to do, your attention to lack negatively impacts you much more than you realize. *A feeling of being overwhelmed is your indicator that you are denying yourself access to ideas, rendezvous, conditions, and all manner of cooperation that could assist you if you were not disallowing them. It is an uncomfortable cycle where you feel a shortage of time, you focus upon your overloaded schedule, and you feel overwhelmed—and in all of that, you offer a vibration that makes improvement impossible.*

You have to begin telling a different story, for you cannot continue to comment on how much you have to do without holding assistance away. There is a cooperative Universe at your fingertips, ready and able to help you in more ways than you can begin to imagine, but you deny yourself that benefit as you continue to complain about too much to do.

As you feel that you do not have enough money, your attention to the lack of money disallows the avenues that could bring you more—you just cannot look at the opposite of what you want and get what you want. You have to begin telling a different story. You have to find a way to create a feeling of abundance before abundance can come.

As you begin to feel freer regarding the expenditure of time and money, doors will open, people will come to assist you, refreshing and productive ideas will occur to you, and circumstances and events will unfold. As you change the way you feel, you access the Energy that creates worlds. It is there for your ready access at all times.

Feeling Negative with Respect to Money or Cancer?

Jerry: So what's the difference between having a negative feeling about money and therefore you *don't* get money and saying, "I don't want cancer," but you *do* get cancer?

Abraham: Here is the way it works: You get the essence of what you think about, and so as you are thinking about the *lack* of health, you are getting the lack of health. As you are thinking about the lack of money, you are getting the lack of money. You can tell by the way you *feel* as you are offering your thought whether you are attracting the positive or the negative aspects of the subject.

The Universe does not hear *no*. When you are saying, *No, I do not want illness,* your attention to the subject of illness is saying, *Yes, come unto me, this thing I do not want.*

Anything you are giving your attention to is an invitation to the essence of it. When you are saying, *I want money, but it will not come,* your attention to its absence is the same as saying, *Come to me, absence of money, which I do not want.*

When you are thinking of money in the way that will make it come to you, you always feel good. When you are thinking of money in the way that keeps it from coming to you, you always feel bad. That is how you know the difference.

So, you are asking, "If I can get cancer by focusing upon the lack of health, then why couldn't I get money by focusing on the lack of it?" The receiving of money, *which you do want,* is the same as the receiving of health, *which you do want.* The receiving of cancer, *which you do not want,* is the same as the receiving of no money, *which you do not want.*

Just make sure that whatever thoughts you are thinking, or whatever words you are speaking, evoke from you positive emotion, and then you will be in the mode of attracting what you *do* want. When negative emotion is present, you are in the mode of attracting something that you *do not* want.

He Didn't Struggle for Money?

[The following is an example of an audience member's question at an Abraham-Hicks workshop.]

Question: I have a friend who had basically financially supported her former husband for about ten years. She worked hard and took care of him for all of that time, often struggling to earn enough money to support them. Eventually she grew tired of his unwillingness to contribute financially, and they separated. Her husband never showed any evidence that money was important to him, but he has now just inherited over a million dollars—and now he will not share his money with his ex-wife (my friend), who supported him for all of those years.

It doesn't seem fair that she cared about money and worked hard for it and received so little, while he barely worked, didn't seem to care about money, and has now inherited over a million dollars. How can this be?

Abraham [the rest of the chapter is Abraham speaking]: Understanding the *Law of Attraction* as we do, this story makes perfect sense. This woman worked hard, felt resentment, focused upon lack—and the Universe matched those *feelings* precisely. Her husband felt ease, refused to feel guilty, expected things to come to him easily—and the Universe matched those *feelings* precisely.

Many believe that they must work hard, struggle, pay a price, and feel pain, and that they will then be rewarded for their struggle—but that is not consistent with the *Laws of the Universe: You cannot find a happy ending to an unhappy journey. That defies Law.*

There is not a shred of evidence to the contrary of the *Law of Attraction;* and you had the benefit of knowing these two people, seeing their attitudes, and watching their results: one struggling, working very hard, doing what society has taught her—and not getting what she wants . . . the other refusing to struggle, insisting on a feeling of ease—and being the recipient of the resources that support more ease.

Many would say, "Well, it might be consistent with the *Laws of the Universe,* but it's still not right," but we want you to know that when you get in sync with this powerful *Law,* you will then understand the absolute justice of it.

Since you have control over what you offer, what could be more just than the Universe giving you exactly what you offer vibrationally? What could be more just than the powerful *Law of Attraction* responding equally to everyone who offers a vibration? Once you gain control over the thoughts you think, your sense of injustice will subside and will be replaced with the exuberance for life and the zest to create that you were born with. *Let everything in the Universe be an example to you of the way the Laws of the Universe work.*

If you believe that you must work hard in order to deserve the money that comes to you, then money cannot come to you unless you do work hard. But the money that comes in response to physical action is very small in comparison with what comes through alignment of thought. Surely you have noticed the enormous disparity between some people who apply tremendous action for little return while you see others seemingly offering very little action for an enormous return. We want you to understand that the disparity exists only in the comparison of the *action* they are offering—but there is no disparity or injustice relative to the *alignment* of Energies within them.

Financial success, or any other kind of success, does not require hard work or action, but it does require alignment of thought. You simply cannot offer negative thought about things that you desire and then make up for it with action or hard work. When you learn to direct your own thoughts, you will discover the true leverage of Energy alignment.

Most of you are much closer to a financial fortune than you are even allowing yourself to purely desire, because, in the thought that it might come, you right away begin thinking of how disappointed you will be if it does *not* come in. And so, in your lackful thought, you do not allow yourself to desire or to expect anything magnificent in terms of money; and that is the reason why, for the most part, you are living rather mediocre financial experiences.

You are right when you think, *Money isn't everything.* You certainly do not need money to have joy in your experience. But in your society—where so much of what you live is tied to money in some way—most of you associate money with freedom. And since freedom is a basic tenet of your Being, then coming into alignment with money will help you establish a balanced footing that will be of value to you in all other aspects of your experience.

Is Spending Money Comfortable?

A very prevalent way of looking at money was expressed to us by a woman who explained that she always feels uncomfortable when she spends her money. She had, over time, managed to save quite a bit of money, but whenever she would think about spending some of it, she would "freeze up" and "feel afraid to go another step further."

We explained: It is certainly understandable that when you believe that your money is coming to you because of the action that you are offering and you also believe that you will not always be able to offer that action, you would want to hold on to your money and spend it sparingly to make it last. However, that feeling of shortage slows the process of more money flowing into your experience.

If you feel uncomfortable with the idea of spending money, then we absolutely do not encourage you to spend the money while you are feeling uncomfortable, because any action taken amidst negative emotion is never a good idea. But the reason for your discomfort is not about the action of spending the money, but instead it is an indication that your thoughts about money in that moment are not a Vibrational Match to your own desire. *A belief in shortage will never resonate with your broader knowing, because there is no shortage. Any attention to lack of something wanted will always produce negative emotion within you because your Guidance is letting you know that you have strayed from your broader basic understanding of abundance and Well-Being.*

Find a way to ease your *discomfort* and eventually transform it into a feeling of hope, and then positive *expectation;* and then from that stable place of feeling better, that feeling of "freezing up" will be replaced with *confidence* and *enthusiasm.* Whether you are focused upon the shortage of *money*—or seeing yourself as having only so many *years* to live (and so each day that is expended is one day closer to the end of your years)—that feeling of decline is contrary to your broader understanding of the Eternal nature of your Being.

In the same way that you understand that you do not have to attempt the impossible task of drawing enough air into your lungs to last all day or all week or all year—but instead you easily breathe in and out, always receiving what you want or need whenever you want or need it—money can flow in and out of your experience with the same ease once you achieve that expectation of Eternal abundance.

All of the money that you want is available for you to receive. All you have to do is *allow* it into your experience. And as the money flows in, you can gently allow it to flow out, for like the air you breathe, there will always be more to flow. You do not have to guard your money (like holding your breath and not letting it out) because there will not be any more coming. More *is* coming.

People sometimes protest as they tell their tales of shortage or scarcity, pointing out the "reality" of the shortage that they have experienced, witnessed, or heard about. And we understand that there are plenty of examples to point to of people who are experiencing shortages of many things that they desire. But we want you to understand that those experiences of shortage are not because abundance is not available, but because it is being *disallowed.*

Continuing to tell stories of shortage only continues to contradict your desire for abundance, and you cannot have it both ways: You cannot focus upon *unwanted* and receive *wanted.* You cannot focus upon stories about money that make you feel uncomfortable and allow into your experience what makes you feel comfortable. You have to begin telling a different story if you want different results.

We would begin by saying, *I want to feel good. I want to feel productive and expansive. My thoughts are the basis for the attraction of all things that I consider to be good, which includes enough money for my comfort and joy, which includes health and wonderful people around me who are stimulating and uplifting and exciting. . . .*

Begin telling the story of your desire, and then add to it the details of the positive aspects that you can find that match those desires. And then embellish your positive expectation by speculating with your good-feeling *Wouldn't it be nice if . . . ?* examples.

Say things like: *Only good things come to me. While I don't have all of the answers, and while I don't know all of the steps, and I can't identify all of the doors that will open for me, I know that as I move through time and space, the path will be obvious to me. I know I will be able to figure it out as I go along.* Every time you tell your better-feeling story, you will feel better and the details of your life will improve. The better it gets, the better it gets.

How to Change My Point of Attraction?

Sometimes people worry that they have been telling the story of what they do not want for such a long time that they now do not have the time left in their lives to make up for all of those years of focusing upon the shortage of money—but they have no cause for worry.

Although it is true that you cannot go backward and undo all of that negative thinking, there is no reason to do that even if you could, because all of your power is in your *now.* As you find a better-feeling thought right now, your point of attraction shifts—now! *The only reason it may seem like some negative thinking that you picked up many years ago is having an impact on your life now is because you have been continuing the negative train of thoughts or beliefs through all of those years. A belief is only a thought you continue to think. A belief is nothing more than a chronic pattern of thought, and you have the ability—if you try even a little bit—to begin a new pattern, to tell a new story, to achieve a different vibration, to change your point of attraction.*

Just the simple act of noticing how many things you could purchase in this one day with the $100 you are carrying with you would dramatically alter your financial point of attraction. That one simple process is enough to tip the balance of your Vibrational Scale enough to show you actual tangible results in your attraction of money. Mentally spend your money and imagine an improved lifestyle. Deliberately conjure a feeling of freedom by imagining what it would feel like to have a large amount of money at your disposal.

You see, the *Law of Attraction* is responding to your vibration, not to the reality you are currently living—but if your vibration continues to be only about the reality you are living, nothing can change. *You can easily change your vibrational point of attraction by visualizing the lifestyle you desire and holding your attention upon those images until you begin to feel relief, which will indicate that a true vibrational shift has occurred.*

My Standards Are Mine to Set

Sometimes from an awareness of a shortage of money, you think that you want everything that you see. A sort of uncontrollable craving rises within you, which tortures you when you do not have the money to spend or causes even more distress when you give in to the craving and spend money you do not have, going deeper into debt. But that craving to spend money under those conditions is really a false signal, for it is not coming from a real desire to have those things. *Buying one more thing and bringing it home will not satisfy that craving, for what you are really feeling is a void that can only be filled by coming into vibrational alignment with <u>who-you-really-are.</u>*

You are currently feeling insecure, when *who-you-really-are* is someone who is absolutely secure. You are currently feeling inadequate, when *who-you-really-are* is someone who is adequate. You are feeling lack, when *who-you-really-are* is someone who is abundant. It is a vibrational shift that you are craving, not the ability to purchase something. Once you are able to achieve and consistently maintain your personal alignment, a great deal of money will flow into your experience (if that is your desire), and you will very likely spend large amounts of money on things that you desire, but your purchases will feel very different to you then. You will not feel need or a void that you are attempting to fill with a purchase, but instead you will feel a satisfying interest in something, which will easily make its way into your experience, and every part of the process— from the inception of the idea to the full-blown manifestation of it into your experience—will bring to you a feeling of satisfaction and joy.

Do not let others set the standards about how much money you should have—or about what you should do with it—for you are the only one who could ever accurately define that. Come into alignment with <u>who-you-really-are,</u> and allow the things that life has helped you to know that you want to flow into your experience.

Does "Saving for Security" Work?

A man related to us that he once had a teacher who told him that to set money aside for security was the same as "planning for a disaster," and in fact the very act of trying to feel more secure would actually lead to more insecurity because it would attract the unwanted disaster. He wanted to know if that philosophy fit in with our teachings about the *Law of Attraction.*

We told him: This teacher was right in pointing out that attention to anything brings more of the essence of it to you, and so if you were to focus upon the idea of possible bad things looming out there in your future, the discomfort that you would feel as you pondered those unwanted things would be your indication that you are, indeed, in the process of attracting them. But it is absolutely possible to briefly consider something unwanted occurring in the future, such as a financial situation that makes you feel insecure as you consider it, which could cause you to then consider the financial *stability* that you *desire.* And as you focus upon the security that you *desire,* you may very well be inspired to an action that enhances that state of security.

The action of saving money, or investing in assets, in and of itself is neither positive or negative, but that teacher would be correct to say that you cannot get to a place of security from an insecure footing. *Our encouragement is to use the power of your mind to focus upon the good-feeling security you seek and then take whatever positive action that is inspired from that place of feeling good. Anything that feels good to you is in harmony with what you want. Anything that feels bad to you is not in harmony with what you want. It is truly as simple as that.*

Some say that you should not want money at all because the desire for money is materialistic and not Spiritual. But we want you to remember that you are here in this very physical world where Spirit has materialized. You are here in your very physical bodies on this very physical planet where that which is Spirit and that which is physical or material blend. *You cannot separate yourself from the aspect of yourself that is Spiritual, and while you are here in these bodies, you cannot separate yourselves from that which is physical or material.*

All of the magnificent things of a physical nature that are surrounding you are Spiritual in nature.

Telling a New Story about Abundance, Money, and Financial Well-Being

The *Law of Attraction* is not responding to the reality that you are currently living and perpetuating, but instead it is responding to the vibrational patterns of thoughts that are emanating from you. So as you begin to tell the story of who you are—in relationship to money—from the perspective of what you *desire* rather than from the perspective of what you are actually currently living, your patterns of thoughts will shift, and so will your point of attraction.

What-is has no bearing on what is coming unless you are continually regurgitating the story of what-is. By thinking and speaking more of how you really want your life to be, you allow what you are currently living to be the jumping-off place for so much more. But if you speak predominantly of what-is, then you still jump off—but you jump off into more of the same.

So consider the following questions, letting your natural answers flow in response to them, and then read some examples of what your new story regarding money might sound like. And then, begin to tell your own new-and-improved story of your financial picture, and watch how quickly and surely circumstances and events will begin to move around you to make your new story a reality:

- Do you have as much money in your life experience as you want right now?

- Is the Universe abundant?

- Do you have the option of having plenty of money?

- Was the amount of money that you would receive in this lifetime already decided before you were born?

- Are you now setting into motion, through the power of your current thought, the amount of money that will flow?

- Do you have the ability to change your financial situation?

- Are you in control of your financial condition?

- Do you want more money?

- Knowing what you now know, is financial abundance guaranteed?

An Example of My "Old" Story about Money

There are so many things that I want that I just can't afford. I'm making more money today than ever before, but money feels as tight as ever. It just seems like I can't get ahead.

It seems like I've worried about money my whole life. I remember how hard my parents worked and my mother's constant worry about money, and I guess I've inherited all of that. But that isn't the kind of inheritance I had hoped for. I know there are really wealthy people in the world who don't have to worry about money, but they aren't anywhere near me. Everyone I know right now is struggling and worried about what's going to happen next.

Notice how this story began by noticing a current unwanted condition; then moved to justification of the situation; then looked into the past for more emphasis of the current problem, which amplified the resentment more; then moved to a broader view of perceived shortage. *When you begin to tell a negative story, the Law of Attraction will help you reach from your present perspective, into your past, even into your future—but the same vibrational pattern of lack will persist. When you focus upon lack in an attitude of complaining, you establish a vibrational point of attraction that then gives you access only to more thoughts of complaint whether you are focused in your present, your past, or your future.*

Your deliberate effort to tell a new story will change that. Your new story will establish a new pattern of thought, providing you with a new point of attraction from your present, about your past, and into your future. The simple effort of looking for positive aspects from right where you stand will set a new vibrational tone that will not only affect the way you feel right now, but will begin the immediate attraction of thoughts, people, circumstances, and things that are pleasing to you.

An Example of My "New" Story about Money

I like the idea that money is as available as the air I breathe. I like the idea of breathing in and breathing out more money. It is fun to imagine a lot of money flowing to me. I can see how my feeling about money affects the money that comes to me. I am happy to understand that with practice I can control my attitude about money, or about anything. I notice that the more I tell my story of abundance, the better I feel.

I like knowing that I am the creator of my own reality and that the money that flows into my experience is directly related to my thoughts. I like knowing that I can adjust the amount of money that I receive by adjusting my thoughts.

Now that I understand the formula for creating; now that I understand that I do get the essence of what I think about; and, most important, now that I understand that I can tell by the way I am feeling whether I am focused upon money or lack of money, I feel confident that in time, I will align my thoughts with abundance—and money will flow powerfully into my experience.

I understand that the people around me hold many different perspectives about money, wealth, spending, saving, philanthropy, giving money, receiving money, earning money, and so forth, and that it is not necessary for me to understand their opinions or experiences. I am relieved to know that I do not have to sort all of that out. It is very nice to know that my only work is to align my own thoughts about money with my own desires about money, and that whenever I am feeling good, I have found that alignment.

I like knowing that it is all right for me to occasionally feel negative emotion regarding money. But it is my intention to quickly direct my thoughts in better-feeling directions, for it is logical to me that thoughts that feel good when I think them will bring positive results.

I understand that money will not necessarily manifest instantly in my experience with the changing of my thinking, but I do expect to see steady improvement as a result of my deliberate effort to think better-feeling thoughts. The first evidence of my alignment with money will be my improved feeling, my improved mood, and my improved attitude—and then real changes in my financial situation will be soon to follow. I am certain about that.

I am aware of the absolute correlation between what I have been thinking and feeling about money and what is actually happening in my life experience. I can see the evidence of the <u>Law of Attraction</u>'s absolute and unerring response to my thought, and I look forward to more evidence in response to my improved thoughts.

I can feel a powerful leveraging of Energy in being more deliberate about my thoughts. I believe, at many levels, that I have always known this, and it feels good to return to my core beliefs about my power and value and worthiness.

I am living a very abundant life, and it feels so good to realize that whatever this life experience causes me to desire—I can achieve that. I love knowing that I am unlimited.

I feel tremendous relief in recognizing that I do not have to wait for the money or the things to materialize before I can feel better. And I now understand that when I do feel better, the things and experiences and money that I want must come.

As easily as air flows in and out of my being—so it is with money. My desires draw it in, and my ease of thought lets it flow out. In and out. In and out. Ever flowing. Always easy. Whatever I desire, whenever I desire, as much as I desire—in and out.

There is no right or wrong way to tell your improved story. It can be about your past, present, or future experiences. The only criterion that is important is that you be conscious of your intent to tell a better-feeling, improved version of your story. Telling many good-feeling short stories throughout your day will change your point of attraction. Just remember that the story *you* tell is the basis of *your* life. So tell it the way you want it to be.

᭔᭔᭔ ᭢᭢᭢

PART III

Maintaining My Physical Well-Being

My Thoughts Create My Physical Experience

The idea of "success," for most people, revolves around money or the acquisition of property or other possessions—but we consider a state of joy as the greatest achievement of success. And while the attainment of money and wonderful possessions certainly can enhance your state of joy, the achievement of a good-feeling physical body is by far the greatest factor for maintaining a continuing state of joy and Well-Being.

Every part of your life is experienced through the perspective of your physical body, and when you feel good, everything you see looks better. Certainly it is possible to maintain a good attitude even when your physical body is diminished in some way, but a good-feeling body is a powerful basis for an ongoing good attitude. And so, it is not surprising that since the way you feel affects your thoughts and attitudes about things, and since your thoughts and attitudes equal your point of attraction, and since your point of attraction equals the way your life continues to play out—*there are few things of greater value than the achievement of a good-feeling body.*

It is quite interesting to note that not only does a good-feeling body promote positive thoughts, but that, also, positive thoughts promote a good-feeling body. That means you do not have to be in a perfect state of health in order to find feelings of relief that eventually can lead to a wonderful mood or attitude, for if you are able to somehow find that relief even when your body is hurting or sick, you will find physical improvement, because your thoughts create your reality.

Complaining about Complaining Is Also Complaining

Many complain that it is easy to be optimistic when you are young and in good health, but that it is very difficult when you are older or sicker . . . but we never encourage using your age or a current state of failing health as a limiting thought that disallows improvement or recovery.

Most people have no idea of the power of their own thoughts. They do not realize that as they continue to find things to complain about, they disallow their own physical well-being. Many do not realize that before they were complaining about an aching body or a chronic disease, they were complaining about many other things first. It does not matter if the object of your complaint is about someone you are angry with, someone who has betrayed you, behavior in others that you believe is wrong, or something wrong with your own physical body—complaining is complaining, and it disallows recovery.

So whether you are feeling good and are looking for a way to maintain that good-feeling state of being or if your physical body is diminished in some way and you are looking for recovery, the process is the same: *Learn to guide your thoughts in the direction of things that feel good, and discover the power that only comes from vibrational alignment with Source.*

As you continue to read this book, things that you have known long before you were born will be remembered, and you will feel a resonance with these *Laws* and processes that will give you a feeling of empowerment. And then all that is required for the achievement and maintenance of a healthy, good-feeling body is some deliberate attention to thoughts and feelings and a sincere desire to feel good.

I Can Feel Good in My Body

If you are not feeling good or looking the way you want to look, it has a way of reflecting out into all other aspects of your life experience, and it is for that reason that we want to emphasize the value in bringing your physical body into balance and comfort and well-being. There is nothing in the Universe that responds faster to your thoughts than your own physical body, and so aligned thoughts bring a quick response and obvious results.

Your physical well-being is really the easiest of subjects over which you have absolute control—for it is what *you* are doing about *you*. However, because you are translating everything in this world through the lens of how your physical body feels, if you do get out of balance, it can negatively affect a much larger part of your life than only your physical body.

You are never more clear about wanting to be healthy and to feel good than when you are sick and feeling bad, and so the experience of being sick is a powerful launching pad for the asking for wellness. So, if, in the moment that your sickness has caused you to ask for wellness, you could turn your undivided attention to the idea of being well, it would occur immediately—but for most, now that you are feeling bad, *that* is what has your attention. *Once you are sick, it is logical that you would now notice how you feel, and in doing so, you would prolong the sickness . . . but it was not your attention to the lack of wellness that made you sick. Instead, it was your attention to the lack of many things that you desire.*

Chronic attention to unwanted things holds you in a place of disallowing your physical well-being, as well as disallowing the solutions to other subjects you are focused upon. *If you could focus your attention upon the idea of experiencing physical well-being with as much passion as you focus upon the absence of it, not only would your recovery come quickly, but maintaining your physical well-being and balance would also be easy.*

Words Do Not Teach, but Life Experience Does

Simply hearing words, even when they are perfect words that accurately explain truths, does not bring understanding, but the combination of careful words of explanation, coupled with life experience that is always consistent with the <u>Laws of the Universe,</u> does bring understanding. It is our expectation that as you read this book and live your life, you will achieve a complete understanding of how all things occur in your experience and you will accomplish complete control of all aspects of your own life, especially things that have to do with your own body.

Perhaps your physical condition is exactly as you want it to be. If that is the case, then continue to focus upon your body as it is, feeling appreciation for the aspects that are pleasing you—and you will maintain that condition. But if there are changes that you would like to make, whether it is in appearance or stamina or wellness, then it will be of great value for you to begin telling a different story—not only about your body, but about all subjects that have been troubling to you. As you begin to positively focus, getting to feel *so* good about so many subjects that you often feel passion rise within you, you will begin to feel the power of the Universe—the power that creates worlds—flowing through you.

You are the only one who creates in your experience—no one else. Everything that comes to you comes by the power of your thought.

When you focus long enough that you feel passion, you harness more power and you achieve greater results. The other thoughts, while they are important and have creative potential, usually are only maintaining what you have already created. And so, many people continue to maintain unwanted physical experiences simply by offering consistent—not powerful, and not accompanied by strong emotion—thoughts. In other words, they merely continue telling the same stories about things that seem unfair, or unwanted things that they disagree with, and in doing so, they maintain unwanted conditions. *The simple intention of telling better-feeling stories about all subjects that you focus upon will have a great effect on your physical body. But since words do not teach, it is our suggestion that you try telling a different story for a while and observe for yourself what happens.*

The *Law of Attraction* Expands My Every Thought

The *Law of Attraction* says that *that which is like unto itself, is drawn.* In other words, that which you think, in any moment, attracts unto itself other thoughts that are like it. That is why whenever you are thinking about a subject that is not pleasant, more unpleasant thoughts regarding that subject are quickly drawn. You find yourself, in very short order, not only experiencing what you are experiencing in *this* moment, but reaching into your past for more data that matches that vibration—and now, by the *Law of Attraction,* as your negative thought expands proportionately, so does your negative emotion.

Soon you find yourself discussing the unpleasant subject with others, and now *they* add to it, often reaching into *their* past . . . until, *in a very short period of time, most of you, upon any subject that you ponder very long, attract enough supporting data that it does bring forth the essence of the subject of the thought into your experience.*

It is natural that by knowing what you *do not want,* you are able to clarify what you *do want;* and there is nothing wrong with identifying a problem before beginning to look for a solution. But many people, over time, become problem oriented rather than solution oriented, and in their examination and explanation of the problem, they continue the perpetuation of the problem.

Again, a telling of a different story is of great value: Tell a solution-oriented story instead of a problem-oriented story. *If you wait until you are sick before you begin to try to focus more positively, it is much harder than if you begin to tell the story of Well-Being from your place of feeling good . . . but, in any case, your new story will, in time, bring you different results. That which is like unto itself, is drawn—so tell the story you want to live and you will eventually live it.*

Some people worry that since they are already sick, they cannot now be well because their sickness now has their attention, and therefore their attention to sickness is perpetuating more sickness. We agree. That would be correct if they only have the ability to focus upon *what-is* at this time. But since it is possible to think about things other than what is happening right now, it is possible for things to change. However, you cannot focus only upon current problems and get change. You have to focus upon the positive results you are seeking in order to get something different.

The <u>Law of Attraction</u> is responding to your thought, not to your current reality. When you change the thought, your reality must follow suit. If things are going very well for you right now, then focusing upon what is happening now will cause the well-being to continue, but if there are things that are happening now that are not pleasing, you must find a way of taking your attention away from those unwanted things.

You have the ability to focus your thoughts—about yourself, about your body, and about the things that matter to you—in a different direction from only what is happening right now. You have the ability to imagine things that are coming or to remember things that have happened before, and when you do so with the deliberate intent of finding good-feeling things to think and speak about, you can quickly change your patterns of thought, and therefore your vibration, and eventually . . . your life experience.

15 Minutes to My Intentional Well-Being

It is not easy to imagine a healthy foot when your toe is painfully throbbing, but it is of great value for you to do everything you can do to distract yourself from your throbbing toe. However, a time of acute physical discomfort is not an effective time to try to visualize well-being. The best time to do that is when you are feeling the best you usually feel. In other words, if you usually feel physically better during the first part of the day, choose that time for the visualization of your new story. If you usually feel best after taking a long, warm bath, choose *that* time for visualization.

Set aside approximately 15 minutes where you can close your eyes and withdraw as much as possible from your awareness of *what-is*. Try to find a quiet place where you will not be distracted, and imagine yourself in a state of physical thriving. Imagine walking briskly and breathing deeply and enjoying the flavor of the air you are breathing. Imagine walking briskly up a gentle incline, and smile in appreciation of the stamina of your body. See yourself bending and stretching and enjoying the flexibility of your body.

Take your time exploring pleasant scenarios with the sole intent of enjoying your body and appreciating its strength and stamina and flexibility and beauty. *When you visualize for the joy of visualizing rather than with the intention of correcting some deficiency, your thoughts are more pure and therefore, more powerful. When you visualize to overcome something that is wrong, your thoughts are diluted with the lackful side of the equation.*

Sometimes people explain that they have long-held desires that have not manifested, and they argue that the *Law of Attraction* is not working for them—but that is because they have been asking for improvement from a place of keen awareness of the lack of what they desire. It takes time to reorient your thoughts so that they are predominantly focused toward what you want, but in time it will feel perfectly natural to you to do so. In time, your new story will be the one that you tell most easily.

If you do take the time to positively imagine your body, those good-feeling thoughts will become dominant, and then your physical condition must acquiesce to those thoughts. If you only focus upon the conditions as they exist, nothing will change.

As you imagine and visualize and verbalize your new story, in time you will *believe* the new story, and when that happens, the evidence will flow swiftly into your experience. A belief is only a thought you continue to think, and when your beliefs match your desires, then your desires must become your reality.

Nothing stands between you and anything that you desire other than your own patterns of thought. There is no physical body, no matter what the state of decline, no matter what the conditions, that cannot achieve an improved condition. Nothing else in your experience responds as quickly as your own physical body to your patterns of thought.

I Am Not Bound by Others' Beliefs

With a little bit of effort focused in the right direction, you will achieve remarkable results, and in time, you will remember that you can be or do or have anything that you focus upon and achieve vibrational alignment with.

You came into your physical body and into this physical world from your Non-Physical perspective, and you were very clear about your intention to be here. You did not define all of the details of your physical life experience before you got here, but you did set forth clear intentions about the vitality of your physical body from which you would create your life experience. You felt enormous eagerness to be here.

When you first arrived in your small infant body, you were closer to the Inner World than to the physical world and your sense of Well-Being and strength was very strong, but as time passed and you became focused more into your physical world, you began to observe others who had lost their strong Connection to Well-Being, and—bit by bit—your sense of Well-Being began to fade as well.

It is possible to be born into this physical world and continue to maintain your Connection to *who-you-really-are* and to your absolute Well-Being; however, most people, once they are focused into this time-space reality, do not. The primary reason for the fading of your awareness of personal Well-Being is the clamoring of those around you for you to find ways to please them. *While your parents and teachers are, for the most part, well-meaning people, they are nevertheless more interested in your finding ways to please them than in your finding ways to please yourself. And so, in the process of socialization, almost all people in almost all societies lose their way because they are coaxed or coerced away from their own Guidance System.*

Most societies demand that you make your action your top priority. You are rarely encouraged to consider your vibrational alignment or your Connection to your Inner World. Most people eventually become motivated by the approval or disapproval that is directed at them by others—and so, with their misplaced attention upon accomplishing the action that is most respected by the onlookers of their lives, they lose their alignment, and then everything in their experience is diminished.

But you were eager about being born into this physical world of such amazing variety because you understood the value of that contrast from which you would build your own experience. You knew that you would come to understand, from your own experience, what you preferred from the variety of options that would be available to you.

Whenever you know what you *do not want,* you understand more clearly what it is that you *do want.* But so many people take that first step of identifying what is *not* wanted, and instead of then turning toward what *is* wanted and achieving vibrational alignment with that, they instead continue to talk about what they do *not* want—and, in time, the vitality that they were born with wanes.

There Is Time Enough to Accomplish It

When you do not understand the power of thought and you do not take the time to align your thought to allow this power, you are then resigned to create through the power of your action—which, comparatively, is not much. And so, if you have been working hard with your action to accomplish something and have not managed to achieve it, often you feel overwhelmed or incapable of now making it happen. Some people simply feel they do not have enough time left in their lives to be and do and have the things that they have dreamed of. But we want you to understand that if you will take the time to deliberately align with the Energy that creates worlds, through the power of focusing your thoughts you will discover a leverage that will help you quickly accomplish things that have formerly seemed not possible.

There is nothing that you cannot be or do or have once you accomplish the necessary alignment, and when you do, your own life experience will give you the evidence of your alignment. Before things actually manifest, your proof of alignment comes in the form of positive, good-feeling emotion; and if you understand that, then you will be able to hold steady to your course while the manifestations of the things you desire are making their way to you. The *Law of Attraction* says: *That which is like unto itself, is drawn. Whatever your state of being—whatever the way you feel—you are attracting more of the essence of that.*

To want or desire something always feels good when you believe you can achieve it, but desire in the face of doubt feels very uncomfortable. We want you to understand that wanting something and believing you can accomplish it is a state of alignment, while wanting something and doubting it is misalignment.

Wanting and believing is alignment.
Wanting and expecting is alignment.
Expecting something unwanted is not alignment.
You can *feel* your alignment or misalignment.

Why Do I Want Perfect Bodily Conditions?

Although it may seem strange to you, we cannot begin to address your physical body without addressing your Non-Physical roots and your Eternal Connection to those roots, because you, in your physical body, are an extension of that *Inner Being*. In very simple terms, in order to be at your maximum state of health and Well-Being, you must be in vibrational alignment with your *Inner Being*—and in order to do that, you must be aware of your emotions or feelings.

Your physical state of well-being is directly related to your vibrational alignment with your *Inner Being* or Source, which means every thought that you think on every subject can positively or negatively affect that Connection. In other words, it is not possible to maintain a healthy physical body without a keen awareness of your emotions and a determination to direct your thoughts toward good-feeling subjects.

When you remember that feeling good is natural and you make an effort to find the positive aspects of the subjects that you are considering, you will train your thoughts to match the thoughts of your <u>Inner Being,</u> and that is of tremendous advantage to your physical body. When your thoughts are chronically good-feeling—your physical body will thrive.

Of course, there is a broad range of emotions—from those that feel very bad to those that feel very good—but in any moment in time, because of whatever you are focused upon, *you actually only have two choices in emotion: a <u>better-feeling one</u> or a <u>worse-feeling one.</u>* So you could accurately say there are really only two emotions, and you effectively utilize your *Guidance System* when you deliberately choose the better-feeling of those two options. And, in doing so, in time you can tune yourself to the precise frequency of your *Inner Being*—and when you do that, your physical body will thrive.

I Can Trust My Eternal *Inner Being*

Your *Inner Being* is the *Source* part of you that continues to evolve through the thousands of life experiences that you live. And with each sifting and sorting experience, the Source within you always chooses the best feeling of the available choices, which means your *Inner Being* is eternally tuning itself to *love* and *joy* and all that is good. That is the reason that when you choose to love another or yourself rather than find fault, you feel good. Good feeling is confirmation of your alignment with your Source. When you choose thoughts that are out of alignment with Source, which produces an emotional response like *fear* or *anger* or *jealousy,* those feelings indicate your vibrational variance from Source.

Source never turns away from you but offers a steady vibration of Well-Being, and so when you feel negative emotion, it means that you are preventing your vibrational access to Source and to the Stream of Well-Being. As you begin telling stories about your body and your life and your work and the people in your life that feel good as you tell them, you will achieve a steady Connection with that Stream of Well-Being that is ever flowing to you. And as you focus upon the things that you desire, feeling positive emotion as you focus, you access the power that creates worlds and you flow it toward your object of attention.

What Is the Role of Thought in Traumatic Injuries?

Jerry: Are traumatic injuries created in the same way that diseases are created, and can they be resolved through thought? Are they like a breakage of something that happened in a momentary incident as opposed to a long series of thoughts leading up to it?

Abraham: *Whether the trauma to your body seemed to come suddenly as a result of an accident or whether it came from a disease such as cancer, you have created the situation through your thought—and the healing will come through your thought as well.*

Chronic thoughts of *ease* promote wellness, while chronic *stressful* or *resentful* or *hateful* or *fearful* thoughts promote disease, but whether the result shows up suddenly (as in falling and breaking your bones) or more slowly (as in cancer), *whatever you are living always matches the balance of your thoughts.*

Once you have experienced the diminishment of Well-Being, whether it has come as broken bones or internal diseases, it is not likely that you will suddenly find good-feeling thoughts that match those of your *Inner Being.* In other words, if before your accident or disease you were not choosing thoughts that aligned with Well-Being, it is not likely that now that you are faced with discomfort or pain or a frightening diagnosis, you will now suddenly find that alignment.

It is much easier to achieve great health from moderate health than to achieve great health from poor health. However, you can get to wherever you want to be from wherever you are if you are able to distract your attention from the unwanted aspects of your life and focus upon aspects that are more pleasing. It really is only a matter of focus.

Sometimes a frightening diagnosis or traumatic injury is a powerful catalyst in getting you to focus your attention more deliberately on things that do feel good. In fact, some of our best students of Deliberate Creation are those who have been given a frightening diagnosis where doctors have told them that there is nothing more that can be done for them, who now (since they have no other options) deliberately begin to focus their thoughts.

It is interesting that so many people will not do what really works until all other options have been exhausted, but we do understand that you have acclimated to your action-oriented world, and so action does seem to most of you to be the best first option. *We are not guiding you away from action, but instead encouraging that you find better-feeling thoughts first, and then follow with the action that you feel inspired to.*

Could a Congenital Illness Be Vibrationally Resolved?

Jerry: Can a *congenital illness*—something a person came into physical form with at birth—be resolved by thought?

Abraham: Yes. From wherever you stand, you can get to wherever you want to be. If you could understand that your *now* is only the jumping-off place for that which is to come, you could move quickly (even from dramatic unwanted things) to things that please you.

If this life experience contains the data that causes you to give birth to a desire, then the wherewithal to accomplish it is available to you. But you must focus upon where you want to be—not where you are—or you cannot move toward your desire. However, you cannot create outside your own beliefs.

Major Diseases Come and Go, but Why?

Jerry: In my earlier years, there were major diseases (tuberculosis and polio) that we hear very little of anymore. But we're not short of diseases, because now we have heart disease and cancer, which we almost never heard of back then. In those days syphilis and gonorrhea were constantly in the news. We don't hear much of those, but now AIDS and herpes stay foremost in the news. Why do there always seem to be more diseases cropping up? As cures are being discovered, why don't we finally run out of diseases *to* cure?

Abraham: Because of your attention to lack. Feelings of powerlessness and vulnerability all produce more to feel powerless and vulnerable about. You cannot focus upon the conquering of disease without giving your attention to disease. But it is also very important to understand that looking for cures for diseases, even when you find them, is a shortsighted and, in the long run, ineffective process because, as you have pointed out, new diseases are continually being created. *When you begin to look for and understand* *the <u>vibrational causes</u> for diseases rather than looking for <u>cures,</u> then you will come to the end of the pile of diseases. When you are able to deliberately accomplish the emotion of ease and its accompanying vibrational alignment, it is possible to live disease free.*

Most people spend very little time basking in appreciation for the wellness they are currently experiencing, but instead they wait until they are sick and then they turn their attention to recovery. Good-feeling thoughts produce and sustain physical well-being. You live in very busy times, and you find many things to fuss and worry about; and in doing so, you hold yourself out of alignment—and disease is the result. And then you focus upon the disease and perpetuate more disease. But you can break the cycle at any time. You do not have to wait for your society to understand in order to achieve wonderful physical wellness yourself. *Your natural state is one of wellness.*

I've Witnessed My Body Heal Itself Naturally

Jerry: I became aware early in life that my body heals quickly. If I cut or scratched my body, I could almost watch it heal right before my eyes. Within five minutes, I could see that healing had begun, and then in a very short time, the wound would be completely healed.

Abraham: Your body is made up of intelligent cells that are always bringing themselves into balance, and the better you feel, the less you are vibrationally interfering with the cellular rebalancing. If you are focused upon things that are bothering you, the cells of your body are hindered in their natural balancing process—and once an illness has been diagnosed and you then turn your attention to that illness, the hindering is greater still.

Since the cells of your body know what to do to come into balance, if you can find a way of focusing your attention upon good-feeling thoughts, you will stop your negative interference and your recovery will come. Every dis-ease is caused by vibrational discord or resistance, without exception, and since most people were unaware of their discordant thoughts prior to the illness (usually making little effort to practice good-feeling thoughts), once the illness occurs it is very difficult to then find pure, positive thoughts.

But if you could understand that your thoughts and your thoughts alone are causing the resistance that is preventing the wellness—and you could turn your thoughts in a more positive direction—your recovery could be very fast. No matter what the disease is, and no matter how much it has progressed, the question is: *Can you direct your thoughts positively regardless of the condition?*

Usually at this point someone asks, "But what about the sick child who has just been born?" Do not assume because a child is not yet speaking that the child is not thinking or offering vibration. There are tremendous influences to wellness and sickness that occur even when the child is still in the womb or is newly born.

By Attention to Wellness, I'll Maintain Wellness?

Jerry: Because I've seen my body heal, and because that healing has been visible to me, I expect that. But how can we get to the point that we *know* that *all* parts of the body will heal? People seem to be most frightened of the parts they can't see—those hidden inside of the body, so to speak.

Abraham: It is a wonderful thing to see the results of your thoughts out in the open in an obvious fashion, and just as your wound or sickness is evidence of misalignment, your healing or wellness is evidence of alignment. *Your tendency toward wellness is much stronger than your tendency for illness, and that is the reason that even with some negative thinking, most of you do remain mostly well.*

You have come to *expect* your wounds to heal, which helps tremendously in the healing process, but when the evidence of your illness is something that you cannot see—where you must rely on the investigation of your doctor who uses his medical tests or equipment to probe for information—you often feel powerless and fearful, which not only slows the healing process, but also is a strong reason for the creation of illness. Many people have come to feel vulnerable about the unseen parts of their bodies, and that feeling of vulnerability is a very strong catalyst in the perpetuation of illness.

Most people go to the doctor when they are sick, asking for information about what is wrong, and when you look for something wrong, you usually find it. *The Law of Attraction insists on it, actually. A continual searching for things wrong with your body will, in time, produce evidence of something wrong, not because it was lurking there all along and you finally probed long enough to find it, but because repeated thought eventually creates its equivalent.*

When Inspired to Visit a Medical Doctor?

Abraham: There are many who would protest our perspective, claiming that we are irresponsible when we do not encourage regular checkups on the quest for things that have gone wrong, or are getting ready to go wrong, or could potentially go wrong, with your physical body. And if we did not understand the power of your thoughts, we might even say that if it makes you feel more secure to go to the doctor, then by all means go.

In fact, sometimes when you go looking for trouble and do not find it, you do feel better. But more often than not, the repeated looking for something wrong over time creates it. It is really that simple. We are not saying that medicine is bad or that there is no value to be received by a visit to your doctor. Medicine, doctors, and all healing professions in general are neither good nor bad at their own face value, but instead they are as valuable as your vibrational stance can allow them to be.

Our encouragement is that you pay attention to your emotional balance, work deliberately to find the best-feeling thoughts you can find, and practice them until they are habitual . . . and, in doing so, you will tend to your vibrational alignment first—and then follow through with whatever action you feel inspired to. In other words, a trip to your doctor—or action toward anything—when accompanied by *joy* or *love* or good-feeling emotion, is always valuable; while action that is motivated by your *fear* or *vulnerability,* or any bad-feeling emotion, is never valuable.

Your physical well-being, like everything else, is profoundly affected by the *beliefs* that you hold. Usually when you are younger, your expectation of wellness is stronger, but as you get older most of you degenerate on a sort of sliding scale that reflects what you are seeing in others around you. And, your observation is not inaccurate. *Older people often do experience more illness and less vitality. But the reason for the decline of people as they get older is not because their physical bodies are programmed to break down over time, but because the longer they live, the more they find to fuss and worry about, causing resistance to their natural Stream of Well-Being. Illness is about resistance, not about age.*

Euphoria in the Jaws of a Lion?

Jerry: I heard that a famous man, Dr. Livingstone, while in Africa, was dragged off by a lion that grabbed him with its jaws. He said that he went into a sort of euphoric state and felt no pain. I've seen prey go limp like that when they're about to be eaten by a larger animal. It's kind of like there is a giving up and the struggle is over. But my question is about his statement about feeling no pain: Was what he was calling *euphoria* a mental condition or a physical condition? And is it something that only happens in extreme conditions like when you're about to be eaten or killed, or could it be utilized by anyone when there is something that's painful in order not to feel the pain?

Abraham: First, we will say that you cannot accurately separate that which is physical from that which is mental from that which is coming from your Higher or *Inner* Being. In other words, you are a physically focused Being, *yes;* and you are a thinking, mental Being, *yes;* but the Life Force or Energy that comes forth from within you is offered from a Broader Perspective. In such a situation where it is likely that you would not recover—in other words, once a lion has you in his jaws (usually, *he* is going to be the victor)—*your Inner*

Being intervenes and offers a flow of Energy that would be received by you as that sort of euphoric state.

You do not have to wait until you are in such an intense situation before you have access to the Stream of Well-Being from Source, but most people do not allow it until they have no other choice. You were right in your choice of words that there was a *giving up* that allowed that Stream of Well-Being to flow powerfully. But we want you to understand that what was actually "given up" was the *struggle,* the resistance—not the *desire* to continue to live in this physical body. You have to take all of that into consideration as you are examining specific situations. Someone with less enthusiasm for life, with less determination to live and continue to accomplish, may very well have experienced a different outcome and have been killed and devoured by the lion. *Everything that you experience is about the balance of thought between your desires and your expectations.*

A state of *allowing* is something that must be practiced in normal day-to-day circumstances, not in the midst of attacks by lions. But even in the middle of such an intense situation, the power of your intentions always causes the outcome. Practiced alignment—brought about by consistently good-feeling thoughts—is the path to being pain free. Pain is only a more emphatic indicator of resistance. First there is negative emotion, then more negative emotion, then more negative emotion (you have tremendous leeway here), then sensation, then pain.

We tell our physical friends: If you have negative emotion and you do not realize that it is an indicator letting you know about resistant thought and you do not do something to correct your resistant thought, by the *Law of Attraction* your resistant thought will grow stronger. If you still do not do anything to bring yourself into alignment and better-feeling thoughts, it will grow stronger still, until eventually you will experience pain and illness or other indicators of your resistance.

How Could Someone Feeling Pain Focus Elsewhere?

Jerry: Okay, so I've heard you say that in order to heal ourselves, we want to get our thoughts off of the problem and onto what we're wanting. But if we're in pain, how can we not feel it? How can we get our attention off the pain long enough to concentrate on something we do want?

Abraham: You are right. It is very difficult not to think about the "throbbing toe." Most of you do not think clearly about what you *do* want until you are living what you *do not* want. Most of you sort of drift into your day, blundering here and there, not offering any real conscious thought. Because you do not understand the power of your thought, you usually do not offer any really deliberate thought until you are faced with something that you do not want. And then, once you are faced with something that you do not want, then you attack it fully. Then, you give it your attention, which—knowing the *Law of Attraction,* as we do—only makes things worse. . . . And so, our encouragement would be: *Look for times (or segments) when you are not feeling such intensity of throbbing pain—and then focus upon the Well-Being.*

You have to find a way of separating what is happening in your experience from your emotional response to what is happening. In other words, you could have pain in your body and during the pain you could be feeling *fear,* or you could have pain in your body while feeling *hopeful.* The pain does not have to dictate your attitude or the thoughts that you are thinking. It is possible to think about something other than the pain. And if you can achieve that, then in time the pain will subside. However, if once the pain occurs, you give the pain your undivided attention, then you will only perpetuate more of what you do not want.

Someone who has been focusing negatively upon any variety of subjects and *now* is experiencing pain, now has to overcome the pain *and* focus positively. You see, your negative habit of thought brought about the illness, and to suddenly switch to the positive thought required to allow wellness is not likely to be a fast process, because now you have the hindering pain or illness, or both, to contend with. *Preventive wellness is far easier to accomplish than cor-rective wellness, but, in either case, improved-feeling thoughts—thoughts of greater and greater relief—are the key.*

Even in situations where a lot of pain is being experienced, there are times of greater and lesser discomfort. Choose the best-feeling times from the range you are experiencing to find positive aspects and to choose better-feeling thoughts. And as you continue to reach for thoughts that bring greater emotional relief, that positive leaning will eventually bring you back to Well-Being—every time, no exceptions.

My Natural State Is One of Well-Being

Abraham: At the core of that which you are is wellness and Well-Being, and if you are experiencing anything less than that, there is resistance present within your vibration. *Resistance* is caused by focusing upon the lack of what is wanted. . . . *Allowing* is caused by focusing upon what is wanted. . . . *Resistance* is caused by thought that does not match the perspective of your Source. . . . *Allowing* is experienced when your current thoughts *do* match the perspective of your Source.

Your natural state is one of wellness, one of absolute health, one of perfect bodily conditions—and if you are experiencing anything other than that, it is only because the balance of thought within you is toward the lack of what you want instead of what you do want.

It is your resistance that causes an illness in the first place, and it is your resistance to illness that holds it to you once it is there. It is your attention to what you do *not* want that creates unwanted things in your experience, and so it is logical that your attention to what you *do* want would be appropriate.

Sometimes you think you are thinking about being well, when you are really worried about being sick. And the only way to be sure of the vibrational difference is by paying attention to the emotion that always accompanies your thought. *Feeling your way to the thoughts that promote wellness is much easier than trying to think yourself there.*

Make a commitment to yourself to feel good and then guide your thoughts accordingly, and you will discover that without even realizing it you have been harboring resentments, feeling unworthy, and feeling powerless. But now that you have decided to pay attention to your emotions, these resistant, illness-producing thoughts will no longer go unnoticed. It is not natural for you to be sick, and it is not natural for you to harbor negative emotion—for, at your core, you are like your *Inner Being: You are well; and you feel very, very good.*

But Could a Baby's Thoughts Attract Disease?

Jerry: How could a new baby attract a disease that it doesn't have a conscious awareness of yet?

Abraham: First, we want to state unequivocally that no one is creating your reality other than you, but it is important to realize that the "you" that you know as you did not begin as that small infant born to your mother. You are an Eternal Being, having lived many experiences, who came forth into this physical body from a long background of creating.

People often think that it would be a much better world if all newborn babies could be born meeting all of the standards of a "perfect" physical body, but that is not necessarily the intention of every Being who comes forth into a physical body. There are many Beings who, because the contrast creates an interesting effect that proves valuable in many other ways, deliberately intend to vary from what is "normal." In other words, you just cannot assume that something has gone wrong when babies are born with differences.

Imagine an athlete who has become very good at playing tennis. People sitting courtside watching the match may assume that this player would be happiest always playing against an opponent with less skill whom she can easily beat, but the athlete may very well prefer exactly the opposite: She may prefer people who are at the top of their game, who draw forth from her focus and precision that has not been drawn before. And, in like manner, *many who are at the top of their game in physical creating want opportunities to view life differently so that new options can be evoked and new experiences can be lived. And these Beings also understand that there can be tremendous benefit to those others who are close by when something different from what is "normal" is being experienced.*

People often incorrectly assume that since the baby cannot speak, it could not be creating its own reality, but that is not the case. Even those who do have language are not creating through words, but through thoughts. Your babies are thinking when they are born, and before they are born they are vibrationally aware. Their vibrational frequencies are immediately affected by the vibrations that surround them in their birth environment, but there is no need to worry about them, for they, like you, were born with a *Guidance System* to help them to discern the difference between the offering of beneficial thoughts and the disallowing of Well-Being thoughts.

Why Have Some Been Born with Illnesses?

Jerry: You speak of the "balance of thought," but are you saying balance of thought even from before we're born? Is that why someone can be born with a physical problem?

Abraham: It is. Just as the balance of your thought now is equaling what you are living, the balance of thought that you held prior to your birth is also what has equaled what you are living. But you must understand that there are those who have come forth deliberately wanting physical "disability" because they wanted the benefit that they knew would come from it. They were wanting to add some balance to their perspective.

Before you came into this physical body, you understood that from wherever you stand, you can make a new decision about what you want. And so, there was no concern about your starting place in your physical body because you knew that if that condition inspired a desire for something different, the new desire was attainable. There are many people who have achieved tremendous success in many areas of life who were born into what would be considered conditions that are the extreme opposite of success. And those raw-and-ragged beginnings served them extremely well, because born out of that poverty or dysfunction was strong desire, which was the beginning of the *asking* that was necessary before success could begin to flow to them.

All Beings who come forth into a physical body have full understanding of the body they are coming into, and you may trust that if they come forth, and remain, it was their intention from the Non-Physical to do so. And, without exception, when where you are currently standing causes you to make another decision about what you *now* desire—you have the ability, if you focus your thought, to accomplish the essence of that creation.

Most who are attracting less than wellness are doing so by default. They may very well desire wellness, while the majority of their thoughts are upon subjects that do not support wellness. *It is not a good idea to stand in your perspective and try to evaluate the appropriateness of what anyone else is living because you will never be able to figure it out. But you always know where you stand relative to what you are wanting. And if you will pay attention to what you are thinking and let your thoughts be guided by the feeling that comes forth within you, you will find yourself guiding your thoughts more of the time in the direction of that which will ultimately please you.*

Let's Discuss the Concept of "Incurable" Diseases

Jerry: The most recent of what we call our "incurable" diseases is AIDS, and yet we're now beginning to see AIDS survivors—people who have lived way beyond the time they were told they were going to be able to live. What would you suggest to someone who is already afflicted with AIDS and now wants help?

Abraham: *There is not a physical apparatus, no matter what the state of deterioration, that cannot achieve perfect health. . . .* But that which you *believe* has everything to do with what you *allow* in your experience. If you have been convinced that something is not cur-able—that it is "fatal"—and then you are told that you have it, usually your *belief* will be that you will not survive . . . and you will not.

But your survival has nothing to do with the disease and everything to do with your thoughts. And so, if you say to yourself: *That may be true for others, but it is not so for me, for I am the creator of my experience, and I choose recovery, not death, at this time* . . . you *can* recover.

These words are easily said by us and not so easily heard by those who do not believe in their power to create, but your experi-ence always reflects the balance of your thoughts. *Your experience is a clear indication of the thoughts that you think. When you change the thoughts you are thinking, your experience, or indicator, must change, also. It is <u>Law.</u>*

Focus on Fun to Regain One's Health?

Jerry: Norman Cousins was an author who contracted a disease that was considered to be incurable. (I don't think anyone had ever recovered from it.) But he survived it, and he said he was able to do so by watching a series of humorous television programs. I under-stand that he just watched these programs—and laughed—and the disease went away. What would you say was behind his recovery?

Abraham: His recovery was accomplished because he achieved vibrational alignment with Well-Being. There are two primary fac-tors involved in his finding vibrational alignment: First, *his desire for wellness was dramatically enhanced by his illness;* and second, *the programs he watched distracted him from the illness—the pleasure that he felt as he laughed at the humor of the programs was his indication that his disallowance of Well-Being had ceased.* Those are the two fac-tors required in the creation of anything: <u>*Want*</u> *it and* <u>*allow*</u> *it.*

Usually, once people have focused upon problems and such enough that they have disallowed their Well-Being and they are seriously ill, they then turn their undivided attention to the illness—thus perpetuating it more. Sometimes a doctor can enhance your belief in wellness if he has a process or a remedy that he believes will help you. In that case, the *desire* is amplified because of the illness, and the *belief* is enhanced because of the proposed remedy—but in the case of the supposedly incurable disease, or in the case of the supposedly *curable* disease, the two factors that brought about the healing were the same: *desire and belief.*

Anyone who can come to expect Well-Being can achieve it under any conditions. The trick is to *expect* Well-Being or, as the man in your example did, simply distract yourself from the *lack* of Well-Being.

Did Ignoring the Illness Resolve the Illness?

Jerry: Throughout my adult life, I've never been so sick that I wasn't able to do the work I intended to do that day. In other words, I always felt my work was so important that I didn't consider *not* doing it. I noticed, however, that if I was beginning to feel less than good—like if I was in the beginning stages of a cold or flu—once I got focused on what I needed to do in terms of my work, the symptoms went away. Is that because I was focused upon something that I *wanted?*

Abraham: Because you had a strong *intention* to do your work— and because you enjoyed it when you did it—you had the advantage of a strong momentum toward your Well-Being. So when it seemed that something was detracting from that Well-Being because of some attention to something unwanted, you had only to focus upon your usual intention and your alignment returned quickly—and the symptoms of misalignment faded quickly.

Often you try to accomplish too much through action, and, in doing so, you feel tired or overwhelmed, and those feelings are your indicator that it is time to stop and refresh. But often you push forward in action rather than taking the time to refresh and realign, and that is a very common reason for uncomfortable symptoms to begin to surface.

Most people, when they feel a symptom of sickness, begin to give their attention to the symptom and usually slide rapidly into more discomfort and misalignment. The key is to catch your misalignment early. In other words, whenever you feel negative emotion, that is your signal to reach for a different thought to improve your vibrational balance—but if you do not, your signal will get stronger, until eventually you may feel physical discomfort. But even then, as in the example you just stated, you can still refocus upon something that you desire (taking your attention from whatever has you out of balance) and come into alignment, and the symptoms of sickness must then leave. *There is no condition from which you cannot recover, but it is much easier if you catch it in the early, subtle states.*

Sometimes being sick provides you an escape from something else that you do not want to do, and so, in your environment, there is much *allowing* of sickness for the sake of not having to do something else. But when you begin playing that sort of game with self, you are opening the door to greater and greater and greater sickness.

What's the Effect of Vaccines on Diseases?

Jerry: Since we create our illnesses through thought, then why do *vaccines*—like the one we have for polio—seem to almost put an end to the spread of those particular types of diseases?

Abraham: The illness amplifies your *desire,* and the vaccine amplifies your *belief.* Therefore, you have accomplished the delicate balance of creation: *You want it and you allow it, or believe it—and so it is.*

What about Medical Doctors,
Faith Healers, and Witch Doctors?

Jerry: Well, that would lead me to my next question. People like *witch doctors, faith healers,* and *medical doctors* . . . all of them have the reputation for *healing* some people and for *losing* some of their patients, too. Where do you see the place for such people in thought, or in life?

Abraham: The important thing that they have in common is that they stimulate *belief* in their patients. The first part of the balance of creation has been accomplished because the illness has enhanced the *desire* for wellness, and anything that brings about *belief* or *expectation* will give positive results. When medicine and science stop looking for *cures* and begin to look for *vibrational causes,* or imbalances, they will see a much higher rate of recovery.

If a doctor does not *believe* that you can recover from your illness, your association with that doctor is extremely detrimental. And often, well-meaning doctors will defend their doubt for your recovery by pointing out the odds against it, telling you that it is not likely that you will be an exception. The trouble with that logic—even though it is based on the facts or evidence that medicine and science have come to expect—is that it has nothing to do with you. There are only two factors that have anything to do with your recovery: your *desire* and your *belief.* And this negative diagnosis is hindering your *belief.*

If you have a *strong* desire for recovery, and doctors are giving you no *hope,* it is logical that you would turn to alternative approaches where hope is not only allowed but encouraged, for there is much evidence to show that people can recover from supposedly "incurable" diseases.

Your Physician as a Means to Well-Being

Abraham: Do not condemn your modern medicine, for it has been created because of the thoughts, desires, and beliefs of the members of your society. But we want you to know that you have the power to accomplish anything that you desire, but you cannot look outside of yourself for the validation to do so; your validation will come from within you in the form of emotion.

Seek your vibrational alignment first, and then follow through with inspired action. Let your medical community assist you in your recovery, but do not ask them to do the impossible—do not ask them to give you a cure to compensate for your misalignment of Energy.

Without *asking* there can be no *answering,* and attention to a problem is really an *asking* for a solution, so it is not unusual that doctors would be examining the physical body looking for problems for which they might have a solution. But *looking for problems* is a powerful catalyst for *attracting* them, and so, often well-meaning doctors are instrumental in perpetuating more illness than they are able to find cures for. *We are not suggesting they are not wanting to help you; we are saying their dominant intent, when they examine you, is to find some evidence of something wrong. And since that is their dominant intent—that is more of what they attract than anything else.*

In time, after they have been involved in it for a long period of time, they begin to believe in the fallibility of man. They begin to notice more often what is wrong than what is right, and that is the reason so many of them begin to attract illness into their own experience.

Jerry: So, is that the reason why often doctors can't heal themselves?

Abraham: That is the reason. It is not easy to be focused upon others' negatives without experiencing the negative emotion within your own being—and illness exists because of the allowance of negativity. *One who never experiences negativity will not be sick.*

What Can I Do to Help Them?

Jerry: What's the best thing that I, as an individual, can do for other people who are having physical problems?

Abraham: *You never help others when you allow yourself to be a sounding board for their complaints. Seeing them as you know they want to be is the most valuable thing you can do for them.* Sometimes that means removing yourself from their vicinity because when you are near them, it is difficult not to notice their complaints. You might say to them, "I've learned the power of my attention and thought, and so as I hear you speaking of what I know you don't want, I must tell you that I must remove myself, for I don't want to contribute to your miscreating." Try to distract them from their complaints; try to help them focus upon some positive aspects . . . do your best to imagine their recovery.

You will know when you are of value to anyone when you are able to think about the person and feel good at the same time. When you love others without worry, you are an advantage to them. When you enjoy them, you help them. When you expect them to succeed, you help them. In other words, when you see them as your own <u>Inner Being</u> sees them, then and only then is your association with them to their advantage.

But What If They're in a Coma?

Jerry: From time to time, someone will say, "I have a friend or family member who's in a coma." Is there anything we can do for a loved one who's in an unconscious state?

Abraham: You are communicating with those around you vibrationally even more than with your words, so even though your loved one may show no signs of recognition, it does not mean that your communication is not being received on some level. *You can even communicate with those who have made their physical transition in what you call "death," so do not assume that a seeming unconscious state has barred your communication.*

The primary reason why people remain in a coma or unconscious state is that they are seeking refreshment from the lackful thoughts that have been hindering them. In other words, while they have withdrawn their conscious attention from the details of their normal life, they are in a state of vibrational communication with their own *Inner Being.* It is an opportunity for refreshment and is often a time of decision making where they are actually determining whether they will find their alignment by returning to the Non-Physical or whether they will awaken again back into their physical body. In many regards, it is not very different from being born into their physical body in the first place.

Here is the best attitude for you to hold regarding such people: *I want you to do what is important to you. I approve of whatever you decide. I love you unconditionally. If you stay, I will be ecstatic . . . and if you go, I will be ecstatic. Do what is best for you.* That is the best you can do for them.

Jerry: And so, those people who are in a state like that for many years . . . they're doing what they *want* to do?

Abraham: *Most of them, if it is that length of time, made the decision not to return long ago, and someone in the physical overrode their decision and kept them plugged into a machine, but their Consciousness has long gone and will not return to this body.*

Could I Inherit My Grandmother's Illness?

Jerry: I've heard people say, "I have migraine headaches because my mother had migraine headaches," or "My mother is overweight, my grandmother was overweight, and my children are also over-weight." Do some people inherit physical problems?

Abraham: What appears to be an inherited tendency is usually the *Law of Attraction's* response to the *thoughts* that you learned from your parents. However, the cells of your body are thinking mechanisms, also, and your cells—like you—can learn vibration from those around them. However, when you identify a desire and you find thoughts that feel good—which indicate that you are in vibrational alignment with your *Inner Being* or Source—the cells of your body will quickly align to the vibration of Well-Being that your positive thought has established. The cells of your body cannot develop negative tendencies that lead to disease when you are in alignment with your Source. Your cells can only get out of alignment when *you* are.

Your body is an extension of your thought. Your contagious or "inherited" negative symptoms are supported by your negative thought and could not occur in the presence of chronically positive thoughts no matter what diseases had been experienced by your parents.

Jerry: If I hear my mother speak of her headaches and I accept that, then I can start having headaches myself?

Abraham: *Whether you heard it from your mother or from any other, your attention to something you do not want will, in time, bring the essence of it to you.* The headache is a symptom of resistance to Well-Being, which occurs when you hold yourself in vibrational contradiction to the Well-Being of your *Inner Being.* For example, worrying about work or feeling anger at your government can cause physical symptoms— *you do not have to focus upon a headache to have one.*

Jerry: If I hear my mother complain of headaches and I consciously reject that and say, "That may be for you, but that's not for me," does that protect me to some degree?

Abraham: It is always to your advantage to speak of what you want, but you cannot stay in alignment with *who-you-really-are* and focus upon your mother's headache at the same time. *Speaking of what you do want while looking at what you do not want does not put you into alignment with what you do want. Take your attention from the things you do not want to attract and put it upon the things you do want to attract.* Focus upon some aspect of your mother that causes you to feel good, or focus upon something other than your mother that causes you to feel good.

What Is the Media's Role in Epidemics?

Jerry: I've been hearing in the media recently that there are free flu shots in town for those who want to go and get them. Will that news affect the spread of the flu virus?

Abraham: Yes, it will be of great value to the spread of the flu virus. There is no greater source of negative influence in your environment today than your television. Of course, as in every part of your environment, there is wanted and unwanted, and you do have the ability to focus and therefore to receive value from your television and media—but those sources do bring you a tremendously distorted, imbalanced point of view. They look all around your world for pockets of trouble, shining spotlights upon them and magnifying them and enhancing the trouble with dramatic music and then funneling it into your living rooms, giving you a tremendously distorted picture of the trouble, versus the Well-Being, of your planet.

The constant barrage of medical commercials is a powerful source of negative influence as they explain to you that "one out of every five people has this disease lurking, and you are probably the one." They influence you to give thought, and then they say, "See your physician." And when you go to your physician (remember, the *intent* of the physician is to find something *wrong*), now your negative expectation is born or enhanced. And, with enough of that influence, your body begins to manifest the evidence of those pervasive thoughts. Your medicine is more advanced today than ever before, and yet more of you are sick than ever before.

Remember, to create anything, you have only to give *thought* to it—and then expect it—and it is. They show you the statistics; they tell you the horror stories; they stimulate your thought, and as you are being stimulated by the thought in great detail, you have the emotion: the *dread,* the *fear . . . I do not want that!* And one half of the equation is complete. Then they encourage you to go in for a checkup or to come and get the free flu shots: "Obviously, we know it's an epidemic or we wouldn't be offering the free flu shots," and that completes the *expectation* or the *allowing* part—and now you are in the perfect position for the receiving of the flu or the essence of whatever else it is they are talking about.

You get what you think about whether you want it or not. And so, it is of great value for you to begin practicing your own story about your Well-Being so that when the television presents that frightening story (one that you do not want to live), you can hear their version and feel humor about it rather than fear.

Catch Uncomfortable Sensations While They're Small?

Abraham: The first indication that you are disallowing your physical well-being comes to you in the form of negative emotion. You will not see a breakdown of your physical body at the first sign of negative emotion, but focusing upon subjects that cause a prolonged feeling of negative emotion will eventually cause dis-ease.

If you are unaware that negative emotion indicates the vibrational disharmony that is hindering the level of Well-Being that you are asking for, you may be, like most people, accepting a certain level of negative emotion and feeling no need to do something about it. Most people, even when they feel alarm at the level of negative emotion or stress they are feeling, do not know what to do about it because they believe they are reacting to conditions or circumstances that are outside of their control. And so, since they cannot control those unpleasant conditions, they feel powerless to change the way they feel.

We want you to understand that your emotions come in response to your focus, and under all conditions you have the power to find thoughts that feel slightly better or slightly worse— and when you consistently choose slightly better, the *Law of Attraction* will bring steady improvement to your experience. *The key to achieving and maintaining a physical state of well-being is to notice the indicators of discord in the early stages. It is much easier to refocus your thoughts in the early, subtle stages than after the <u>Law of Attraction</u> has responded to chronic negative thoughts, bringing bigger negative results.*

If you could make a decision to never allow negative emotion to linger within you—and at the same time acknowledge that it is your work alone to refocus your attention in order to feel better rather than asking someone else to do something different or for some circumstance to change to make you feel better—you will not only be a very healthy person, but you will be a joyful person. *Joy, appreciation, love, and health are all synonymous. Resentment, jealousy, depression, anger, and sickness are all synonymous.*

Are Arthritis and Alzheimer's
Disease Somehow Resolvable?

Jerry: Can the gnarled joints caused by arthritis or the memory loss caused by Alzheimer's be resolved? Is it possible to recover from those types of illnesses at whatever age?

Abraham: The conditions of your physical body truly are vibrational indicators of the balance of your thoughts—and so when you change your thoughts, the indicators must change, also. The only reason that some diseases seem stubborn and unchangeable is because your thoughts are often stubborn and unchanging.

Most people learn their patterns of counterproductive thought often based on "truths" they have witnessed or learned from others, and as they hold stubbornly to those patterns of thought (which do not serve them), they then experience the results of those thoughts. And then an uncomfortable cycle occurs where they think about *unwanted* things (valid, true unwanted things) and, in doing so, by the *Law of Attraction,* they prevent *wanted* things from coming into their experience and allow *unwanted* things to come instead—then they focus even more upon those unwanted things, causing more unwanted things to come.

You can accomplish change in every experience, but you have to begin to see your world differently. You have to tell the story the way you want it to be rather than like it is. When you choose the direction of your thoughts and conversations by the way they feel as you think them or speak them, then you begin to *deliberately* offer vibrations. You are Vibrational Beings, whether you know it or not, and the *Law of Attraction* is eternally responding to the vibrations you are offering.

Jerry: Can chemicals, such as alcohol, nicotine, or cocaine, negatively affect the body?

Abraham: *Your physical wellness is affected much more by your vibrational balance than it is by the things that you put into your body. And, even more significant to your question is the fact that from your* *place of vibrational alignment, you would not feel inclined toward any substance that would detract from that balance.* Almost without exception, the seeking of those substances comes from a place of less alignment. *In fact, the impulse to participate in those substances comes from a desire to fill the void that is present because of the vibrational imbalance.*

Are Exercise and Nutrition a Health Factor?

Jerry: Does better nutrition or more exercise add to our health?

Abraham: You may have noticed that there are those who are very deliberate about food and exercise whose physical well-being is obvious. And there are those who seem to be offering tremendous effort regarding food and exercise who struggle for years to gain benefit and still have no success in maintaining their physical well-being. What you do in terms of action is far less important than the thoughts you think, the way you feel, your vibrational balance, or the story you tell.

When you take the time to find vibrational balance, the physical effort you apply will yield you wonderful results, but if you do not tend to your vibrational balance first, there is not enough action in the world to compensate for that misaligned Energy. From your place of alignment, you will feel inspired to the beneficial behavior, just as from your place of misalignment, you are inspired to detrimental behavior.

Jerry: I remember hearing a line from Sir Winston Churchill. (He was the British leader during World War II.) He said, "I never run if I can walk, and I never walk if I can stand, or stand if I can sit, or sit if I can lie down," and he always smoked a big cigar. He lived to be 90 years of age and, as far as I know, was in good health. But his lifestyle was clearly not what we consider today to be healthy, so was it just a *belief* factor then?

Abraham: Leaving at such an early age? (Fun) The reason that so many are confused about the correct behavior for healthy living is because they are only factoring in behavior and they are leaving out the part of the equation that is most responsible for every outcome: the way you think, the emotions you feel, and the story you tell.

What If a Healthy Person Feels Mostly Tired?

Jerry: If a person seems to be in good health but feels tired or listless most of the time, what would you suggest as a solution?

Abraham: People often refer to that state of being tired or listless as a state of low energy, and that is really a good way of saying it. While you cannot cut yourself off from your Energy source, when you offer thoughts that contradict that source, your resulting feeling is one of resistance or low energy. *The way you feel is always about the degree to which you are in alignment or out of alignment with your Source. No exceptions.*

As you tell the story of what you want (which is the story the Source within you is always telling), you feel happy and energized. The feeling of low energy is always a result of telling a different story than the expanded, Source Energy part of you is telling. When you tell a story that focuses upon the positive aspects of your life—you feel energized. When you tell a story that focuses upon the negative aspects—you feel enervated. When you focus upon the absence of something that you desire in your present experience—you feel negative emotion. When you imagine an improved condition—you feel positive emotion. *The way you feel is always about the relationship between the object of your attention and your true desire. Giving thought to what is wanted will give you the invigoration that you seek.*

What Is the Chief Cause of Illness?

Jerry: So in simple terms, what do you see as the chief cause of illness?

Abraham: Illness is caused by giving thought to unwanted topics, feeling negative emotion but ignoring it, and continuing to focus upon *unwanted* such that negative emotion is getting greater—but still ignoring it and maintaining attention upon *unwanted* . . . until, by the *Law of Attraction,* still more negative thoughts and experiences are attracted. *Illness exists when you disregard the early, subtle signs of misalignment that come in the form of emotion.*

If you feel negative emotion and you do not change the thought to relieve the discomfort of the negative emotion, it always gets bigger, until eventually the negative emotion becomes physical sensation—then physical deterioration. *However, the illness is only an indication of your vibration, and whenever you change your vibration, the indicator will change to match the new vibration. Illness is nothing more than a physical indicator of Energy out of balance.*

Many people who are experiencing illness disagree with our explanation of the cause of their illness being that the *Law of Attraction* is responding to their thoughts, as they protest that they have never thought about *that* particular illness. But illness does not occur because you are thinking about *that* illness or about *any* illness. *Illness is an exaggerated indicator of negative thoughts that began as a subtle indicator of negative emotion and grew larger as the negative thoughts persisted. Negative thought is resistance, no matter the subject of the negative thought. That is the reason that new diseases continue to come about, and until the actual cause of the disease is addressed, there will never be a final cure.*

You have potential for every illness in your body right now, and you have potential for a perfect state of health in your body right now—and you will solicit one or the other, or a mixture, depending upon your balance of thought.

Jerry: So, in other words, from your perspective there is no *physical* cause for illness or disease? It's all *thought?*

Abraham: We understand your urge to give credence to action or behavior in attempting to explain causes. As you explain where your water comes from, you would be accurate to point to the faucet as the source of the water coming into your kitchen sink. But there is much more to the story of "where the water comes from" than only the faucet. And in like manner, there is much more to the story about the source of wellness or of illness. *Your ease or dis-ease are symptoms of the balance of your thought, and that balance will manifest through the path of least resistance as surely as water flows downhill.*

An Example of My "Old" Story about My Physical Well-Being

I'm noticing symptoms in my body that worry me. As I get older, I feel less strong, less stable, less healthy, less secure. I worry about where I'm headed healthwise. I've tried to take care of myself, but I don't see that it has helped that much. I guess it's just normal to feel worse as time goes on. I saw that with my parents, so I'm really worried about my health.

An Example of My "New" Story about My Physical Well-Being

My body responds to my thoughts about it and to my thoughts about everything I think about. The better my thoughts feel when I think them, the more I allow my own personal Well-Being.

I like knowing that there is an absolute correlation between how I feel and what my chronic thoughts have been and how those thoughts felt as I thought them. I like knowing that those feelings are meant to help me choose better-feeling thoughts, which produce better-feeling vibrations, which will produce a better-feeling body. My body is so responsive to my thoughts, and that is such a good thing to know.

I am getting rather good at choosing my thoughts. No matter what condition I find myself in, I have the power to change it. My state of physical health is simply an indication of the state of my chronic thoughts—I have control of both.

A physical body is an amazing thing in the way it began as a glob of fetal cells to become this full-blown human body. I am impressed with the stability of the human body and the intelligence of the cells that make up the human body as I notice how my body accomplishes so many important functions without my conscious involvement.

I like that it is not my conscious responsibility to move the blood through my veins or the air through my lungs. I like that my body knows how to do that and does that so well. The human body in general is quite an amazing thing: an intelligent, flexible, durable, resilient, seeing, hearing, smelling, tasting, touching thing.

My own body serves me very well. I love my exploration of life through my physical body. I enjoy my stamina and flexibility. I like living life in my body.

I am so pleased with my eyes that look out into this world, seeing near and far from where I stand, distinguishing shapes and colors with such vivid perception of depths and distances. I so enjoy my body's ability to hear and smell and taste and feel. I love the tactile, sensual content of this planet and my life in my wonderful body.

I feel appreciation and fascination for my body's self-patching ability as I watch wounds cover over with new skin and as I discover renewed resiliency when traumas to my body occur.

I am so aware of my body's flexibility, my fingers' dexterity, and the immediate response that my muscles show to any task I attempt.

I like understanding that my body knows how to be well and is always moving toward wellness, and that as I do not get in the way of that with negative thought, wellness must prevail.

I like understanding the value of my emotions, and I under-stand that I have the ability to achieve and maintain physical well-being because I have the ability to find and maintain happy thoughts.

On any day in this world, even when some things in my body may not be at their best, I am ever aware that far, far, far, far more things are functioning as they should, and that the aspects of Well-Being of my body are dominant.

And most of all, I love my body's quick response to my attention and intentions. I love understanding my mind-body-spirit connections and the powerful productive qualities of my deliberate alignment.

I love living life in my body.

I feel such appreciation for this experience.

I feel good.

There is no right or wrong way to tell your improved story. It can be about your past, present, or future experiences. The only criterion that is important is that you be conscious of your intent to tell a better-feeling, improved version of your story. Telling many good-feeling short stories throughout your day will change your point of attraction. Just remember that the story *you* tell is the basis of *your* life. So tell it the way you want it to be.

ﻌﻔﻌﻔﻌﻔ ﻪﻟﻪﻟﻪﻟ

PART IV

Perspectives
of Health,
Weight, and Mind

I Want to Enjoy a Healthy Body

Bringing your physical body into alignment is a tremendously valuable thing to do for two reasons:

- First, there is no subject that people think more about than their own body. (And that is logical since you take it with you everywhere you go.)

- Second, since every perspective or thought that you have flows through the lens of your physical body, your attitude on virtually every subject is influenced by the way you feel about your physical body.

Because science and medicine have been slow to acknowledge the connection between mind and body, between thoughts and outcomes, and between attitudes and results, most people are reeling in a plethora of contradictory guidance relative to their bodies. *Whenever the basis of an understanding is flawed, no amount of patching it with methods, potions, or remedies can bring consistently provable results. And because the alignment of Energies for each individual varies because of such a variety of factors in beliefs, desires, expectations, and early and current influences, it is little wonder that remedies that "work every time" are nonexistent, and it is no wonder that most are truly confused about their physical bodies.*

When you attempt to gather and process information about what is happening with other people's bodies instead of utilizing your own *Emotional Guidance System* to understand *your* current alignment or misalignment of Energy, it is tantamount to using a road map from a different country to plan your route in your own country: That information simply has no bearing on you and where you are right now.

You have been given so much information that is contradictory to that which we know to be (and to the *Laws of the Universe*) that we are extremely happy to talk to you about you and your body relative to the greater picture. We want to assist you in finding a clear understanding of how to be a healthy Being who is physically fit, who looks as you want to look (whole in terms of mind and spirit and body); and when you use your mind to deliberately focus your thoughts to align with the thoughts of your *Inner Being* (or spirit), your physical body will be the manifestational evidence of that alignment.

I Want to Balance My Desires and Experiences

It is not possible to bring your physical body to a state of perfect health by only thinking about the physical aspects of your being and then offering action regarding your physical body. Without an understanding of the Connection between the physical you and the Non-Physical Vibrational Inner You, there can be no consistent understanding or control. In other words, while it may feel to you that the path to a good-feeling, good-looking body will be a result of your behavior in terms of food intake and activity, it is really much more about your vibrational alignment between the physical and Non-Physical aspects of your being.

Once you accept the totality of your Being and you make that vibrational alignment your top priority, you are well on your way to achieving and maintaining your desired physical body. But if you use conditions of others, experiences of others, and opinions of others as your gauge for wellness, you will not be able to control the condition of your own physical body. In other words, as you strive for a physical standard based on comparison with the experiences of others rather than striving for your personal alignment between you and *You,* you will never discover the key to control over your own body.

I Needn't Compare My Body to Others

We would like to assist you in understanding that there is not one state of being that is the correct one, or even the most wanted one, for there are a great many varieties of states of physical bodies that have been intended by you as you emerged into this physical body. If it had been your intent to all be the same, more of you would be the same—but you are not. You come forth with all sorts of varieties of size and shape and flexibility and dexterity. Some are stronger, and others are more agile. . . . You came with great variety, adding all sorts of differences that are of tremendous advantage to the whole. You came forth in your great variety to add balance to this time and place.

And so, we would like to encourage you: Rather than looking at yourselves and acknowledging that you are lacking in this or in that characteristic, as most of you do, we would like to assist you in looking toward the advantages of that which *you are.* In other words, as you are assessing or analyzing your physical body, spend a greater part of your time looking for the advantages that it offers not just to you, but to the balance of *All-That-Is.*

Jerry: I recall that when I used to work out on a trapeze (with the circus), I was too heavy to be what they called a "flyer," and I was too light to be what they called a "catcher." So the trapeze wasn't my place to be comfortable unless we got a heavier catcher or a lighter flyer, so to speak. So, I was still an *aerialist,* but I performed what was called an aerial bar act, where nobody had to catch me and I didn't have to catch anyone. But I didn't see myself lacking because I didn't think that I should have been bigger or smaller. I just found something I liked to do that still gave me the same general feeling of performing as an aerialist. [**Abraham:** Good. That is excellent.]

What If I Saw Myself as Perfect?

Jerry: So couldn't we look at our weight, then, and our state of mental ability or talent in the same way? Could each of us see ourselves as perfect?

Abraham: We are not necessarily encouraging you to look at whatever your current state is and proclaim it as "perfect," because you will always be striving for something that is just beyond *what-is*. But finding aspects of your current experience that feel good when you focus upon them will cause you to align with the perspective of your *Inner Being,* who is always focused upon your Well-Being. *We encourage you to feel for the agreement between your thoughts about your body and your Inner Being's thoughts about your body rather than trying to get the conditions of your body to agree with conditions of other bodies that you see around you.*

Pushing Against Unwanted Attracts More Unwanted

Abraham: As you are understanding that you are creating through your thoughts rather than through your action, you will accomplish many more of your desires with far less effort—and in the absence of struggle, you will have much more fun. You are offering thought in every waking moment, and so achieving a propensity to positive, good-feeling thoughts will serve you extremely well.

You were born into a society that began warning you against unwanted things as soon as you arrived, and over time, most of you have taken on a guarded stance. You have a "war against drugs" and a "war against AIDS" and a "war against cancer." Most of you really believe that the way to get what you *do* want is to defeat what you *do not* want, and so you give so much of your attention toward pushing away from you what you do not want, where, if you could see the *Law of Attraction* as we see it—if you could accept yourselves as the attractors by virtue of the thought that you are holding—you would understand what a backward approach most of you are taking.

As you say, "I'm sick and I want not to be sick, so I'll beat this illness—I'll take this action and I'll defeat this illness," you are, from your position of guardedness and defensiveness and negative emotion, holding on to that illness.

My Attention to Lack Attracts More Lack

Abraham: Every subject is really two subjects: There is the subject of what you are wanting, and there is the subject of its lack. Regarding your body, since every thought that you think is filtered through your perspective of this body, if this body does not feel the way you want it to feel or look the way you want it to look, it is very natural that a large number of your thoughts (a very imbalanced proportion of your thoughts) would be slanted toward the lack side of the equation rather than toward the truly desired side of the equation.

From your place of lack, you will attract only more of that, and that is the reason most diets do not work: You are aware of your fat—you are aware of your body looking the way you do not want it to look—and so when it gets bad enough that you cannot stand it anymore (either from your own perspective or because others are scowling at you), then you say, "I can't bear this negative place anymore. I'm going to go on a diet, and I'm going to get rid of all of this stuff that I do *not* want." And yet, your attention is given to the stuff that you do not want, and so you hold it to you. *The way to get to where you want to be is to give your full attention to what you <u>do</u> want, not to give your attention to what you <u>do not</u> want.*

Planting Fear Seeds Does Grow More Fear

Jerry: A dear friend, my mentor in business, volunteered to be a part of a medical study. He said that even though he was in brilliant health, he was willing to participate if it could be of value to others, because so many men his age in that area were dying from a certain disease. Well, it seemed like only a matter of weeks before we received a message from him that he had been diagnosed with the illness. And now he's no longer in physical form, but he didn't seem to have a fear of the disease. Did he create it in his body by merely focusing on it?

Abraham: It was his attention to it—in other words, it was his intent to be of value for others. And so, he allowed them to probe and poke and look. And in the probing and poking and looking, he received enough stimulation of thought from the others to make him aware of the possibility—not only the possibility, the *probability. They planted within him the seed of probability, and then, with the probing and the poking and the looking, his body responded to what then became the balance of his thought.*

It is a wonderful example that you have offered because that disease was not within him until the *attention* to the disease was within him, but once the attention to the disease was within him, then his body responded in kind.

The potential for wellness or illness is always within you. The thoughts you choose determine which you experience and to what degree you experience it.

Must Attention to Illness Attract Illness?

Jerry: How much can we toy with these thoughts of illness? For instance, a person can watch on television an offer to come down for a free examination of some part of his or her body, and if the person says, "Oh well, I think I'll just go do that—I feel fine, but why not, since it's free?" what are the chances of that leading to what you're talking about: a stimulation of thought and, eventually, an unwanted result?

Abraham: Nearly 100 percent. Because of the attention to illness in your society, your diseases are running rampant. With all of your medical technology—all of the tools, all of the discoveries— there are more people who are critically ill today than ever before.

The prevalence of so much severe illness is predominantly because of your attention to illness.

You said: "How much can we toy" with it? And we say: You are very particular about what you eat and what you wear and what you drive, and yet you are not particular about what you think. *We would encourage you to be particular about what you think. Keep your thoughts on the side of the subject that is in harmony with your wanting. Think about wellness—not about lack of it. Think about being as you want to be rather than the lack of it.*

Your illnesses are not born and perpetuated only because of your negative attention to illness. Remember that illness stems from your feelings of vulnerability and guardedness. Train your thoughts on all subjects (not only the subject of physical health) in the direction of what you desire, and through the improved emotional state that you accomplish, your physical well-being will then be assured.

Is My Attention Predominantly Focused on Well-Being?

Jerry: Another dear friend of ours recently built a room onto her house so that her mother-in-law, whose health had really worsened, could come to live with her. Her mother-in-law spoke almost constantly about how bad she felt, how bad her health was, how unhappy she was with life, and about this surgery and that surgery.

Then our friend's mother, who was 85 years old, came out to visit for the holidays. She had never been in a hospital in her life before, but within a week of staying in that house with this other lady—who was continually speaking of illness—her own health plummeted dramatically. She was hospitalized and then was placed in a nursing home. Could someone's health fail so dramatically as a result of only a few days of negative influence?

Abraham: *The potential for illness or wellness lies within all of you at all times. And whatever you give your attention to begins to foster within you the manifestation of the essence of that thought. Thought is very powerful.*

While it is not necessary, most people who have lived to be 85 years of age have already been receiving substantial negative influence about their physical body. You are constantly bombarded with thoughts of failing health: a need to buy medical insurance, a need to buy burial insurance, a need to get your will in order to prepare for your death, and so on. So this woman did not receive her first negative influence about her physical well-being from the other woman in that house.

However, since she was already teetering there, somewhat unstable about her own longevity, the intensity of the other woman's conversation—and the responses she noticed that it extracted from the people who surrounded her—did tip the balance of her thoughts enough that negative symptoms became immediately apparent. And then, as she turned her attention toward her own negative symptoms, in that intense environment those symptoms increased even more rapidly.

When someone comes into your experience who stimulates your thought so that your thought is predominantly upon illness rather than wellness, upon lack of Well-Being rather than upon Well-Being, where you are in a place where you are feeling vulnerable or defensive or even angry—then the cells of your body begin to respond to the balance of that thought. And yes, it is possible that in a matter of weeks, or even days—or even hours—this negative process could begin. *Everything that you are living is as a result of the thoughts that you are thinking, and there is not an exception to that.*

Others' Physical Evidence Needn't Be My Experience

Abraham: As you see physical evidence around you, very often that *physical evidence* seems more real to you than a *thought.* You say things to us such as: "Abraham, this is really real—this isn't just a thought," as if what is *really real* and a *thought* are two separate things. But we want you to remember that the Universe does not distinguish between your thoughts of current reality and thoughts of imagined reality. The Universe and the *Law of Attraction* are simply responding to your thought—real or imagined, current or remembered. *Whatever evidence you see around you is nothing more than the manifestational indicator of someone's thought, and there is no reason for what others are creating with their thoughts to cause you to feel frightened or vulnerable.*

There is no such thing as an unchangeable condition. There is not a physical situation, no matter what the state of negative degeneration, that cannot receive wellness. But it requires an understanding of the <u>Law of Attraction,</u> *the guidance represented by emotion, and a willingness to deliberately focus upon things that make you feel good. If you could understand that your body is responding to what you are thinking, and if you could hold your thoughts where you want them to be—all of you would be well.*

How Can I Influence All Toward Maintaining Health?

Jerry: So, what would be the best thing we could do to either maintain or regain perfect health or to influence others around us toward *their* perfect health?

Abraham: Actually, the process for regaining health and maintaining health are one and the same: *Focus upon more things that feel good.* The biggest difference between regaining and maintaining is that it is easier to think good-feeling thoughts when you feel good than when you feel bad, so *maintaining* health is much easier to do than *regaining* health. *The best way to influence others to good health is to live it. The best way to influence others to sickness is to get sick.*

We understand that for those who are now in a place where they do not want to be, it sounds very simplistic to just find a better-feeling thought. But it is our absolute promise to you that if you were to be determined to improve the way you feel by deliberately choosing thoughts that feel better, you would begin to see immediate improvement in anything that is troubling you.

I'll Relax and Sleep Myself into Well-Being

Abraham: Your natural state is one of absolute Well-Being. You do not have to fight anymore against illness. Just relax into your wellness. Put yourself in your bed tonight, and as you are going to sleep, feel the wonderful comfort of the bed beneath you. Notice how big it is. Notice the pillow beneath your neck. Notice the fabric upon your skin. Give your attention to things that feel good, for every moment that you can think about something that feels good, you are cutting the fuel to that illness. *In every moment that you think about something that feels good, you are stopping the illness from going forward; and in every moment that you are thinking about the illness, you are adding a little more fuel to the fire, so to speak.*

As you are able to accomplish holding your thoughts on something that feels good for five seconds, then for that five seconds you will stop fueling your illness. As you accomplish it for ten seconds, then for ten seconds you have stopped fueling the illness. As you think about how good you feel right now, and as you think about your natural state as being a state of wellness—*you begin fueling your wellness.*

Do Negative Emotions Indicate Unhealthy Thoughts?

Abraham: As you think thoughts of illness, the reason you feel such negative emotion about it is because that thought is so out of harmony with your greater knowing that you are not resonating with *who-you-really-are*. The negative emotion that you feel, in the form of *concern* or *anger* or *fear* about your illness, is your real indicator that you have put a very strong restriction on the flow of Energy between you and *who-you-really-are*.

Your wellness comes forth as you allow the full flow of Non-Physical Energy from your *Inner Being*. And so, as you think, *I am well* or *I am becoming well* or *I am whole; it is my natural state to be well,* those thoughts vibrate in a place that is in harmony with that which your *Inner Being* knows to be, and you receive the full benefit of the thought Energy that comes forth from your *Inner Being*.

Every thought vibrates. And so, focus upon thoughts that make you feel good, which will attract others and others and others and others and others . . . until your vibrational frequency will raise to the place that your <u>Inner Being</u> can fully envelop you. And then you will be in the place of Well-Being, and your physical apparatus will catch up very quickly— it is our absolute promise to you. You may begin to watch for dramatic physical evidence of your recovery—for it is <u>Law.</u>

To What Degree Can I Control My Body?

Jerry: Well, this subject is "Perspectives of Health, Weight, and Mind": *How can I get there and stay there?* I see an absolutely overwhelming number of people who are concerned about the state of their weight and their physical and mental health. And because of the amount of attention to physical health failures, I understand why people are concerned.

As a kid, I had the good fortune, somehow, of realizing that I was in control of my own body. I recall when I was about nine years old going to the county-fair carnival, where two professional fighters would take on all comers. In other words, any of the farmers around there could pay to get in the boxing ring and fight them, and if the farmers could beat those professional fighters, they'd win money. But the farmers always got beaten to a pulp. . . .

I remember standing in this little canvas tent lit by kerosene or gas lamps, and I can recall watching the lights flickering on the sweating back of the professional fighter. And I was just absolutely entranced with the fact that his backbone was hidden between two beautiful muscles running down his back, whereas mine was more like our Arkansas state mascot: the razorback hog. In other words, my backbone stuck way out and had no muscles around it, while his was beautifully embedded where I couldn't even see it. I so enjoyed observing these beautiful back muscles. I really appreciated what I saw that day, and within about eight years the muscles on my back did look like that, and so from that experience, I realized that I could create my physical body.

As a result of the extreme ill health that I experienced as a child, I learned somehow to be able to *control* my own health. I experimented with doctors a few times, but their diagnoses and treatments were mostly always wrong. And so, it didn't take me long to realize that I'd be better off staying away from doctors because I couldn't find one I could count on to be right. They were nearly always wrong when it came to helping me, so I decided I'd be better off just handling my own body.

But I still find myself thinking a little bit about how my body is going to hold up and what my future condition is going to be. Will I be able to, as I say, maintain this perfect state of weight, health, and mind? I feel I'm there now, but I'm at the point of sometimes wondering, *Will I be able to always stay there?* And so, I'd like you to address that general subject.

Abraham: We are appreciating the combination of words that you have put there, for your body and your mind are forever connected. *Your body is responding to your thoughts continually—in fact, to nothing else. Your body is absolutely a pure reflection of the way you think. There is nothing else that is affecting your body other than your thoughts.* And it is a good thing that at that early age you proved to yourself that you did have some control over your own body.

When you consciously acknowledge the absolute correlation between what you are thinking and what you are getting, you can then eventually, under all conditions, control your own experience. All that is required for you to get only what you want, versus getting some of what you do *not* want, is to recognize that the control that you seek you already have, and then to deliberately think about things that you want to experience.

Thoughts of decline always feel bad because you do not want decline. So utilize your Guidance and choose good-feeling thoughts and you will have no reason to worry about moving through time. Really, it is simply a matter of making the decision: *I want to acknowledge that I have the only—and the absolute—control of my own physical apparatus. I acknowledge that <u>I am as a result of the thoughts I think.</u>*

The day you were born, you possessed knowledge (not *hope* or *desire,* but deep *understanding*) that your basis is absolute freedom, that your quest is joy, and that the result of your life experience would be growth; and you knew that you are perfect and still reaching out for even more perfection.

Can We Consciously Grow New Muscle and Bone?

Jerry: I consciously, deliberately, added muscle to my body in my early years because I wanted to, but can we consciously affect our bones as well?

Abraham: You can—in the same way. The difference is that the current *belief* about the muscle is there. The current belief about the bone is not.

Jerry: That's true. I saw a man who had developed tremendous muscles, and I wanted that. And because many others were doing it, I believed I could, too. But I haven't seen bone changed.

Abraham: The reason that more things do not change more quickly in your societies today is because most people are giving their attention predominantly to *what-is.* In order to effect change, you must look beyond *what-is.*

It slows you down tremendously if you need to see evidence of something before you believe it, because that means you have to wait for someone else to create it before you can believe it. But when you understand that the <u>Universe,</u> and the <u>Law of Attraction,</u> will respond to your imagined idea as quickly as it responds to an observed idea, then you can move quickly into new creations without having to wait for someone to accomplish it first.

Jerry: So, the challenge is being that "pioneer"—the first one out.

Abraham: The Leading Edge requires vision and positive expectation, but it is really where the most powerful exhilaration is. To be in a state of desire and to have no doubt is the most satisfying experience possible, but to want something and not believe in your ability to achieve it does not feel good. When you think only of what you desire, without constant contradictions that are filled with doubt or disbelief, the Universal response to your desire comes quickly, and in time you begin to feel the power of your deliberate thought. But that kind of "pure" thought takes practice, and it requires that you spend less time observing *what-is,* and more time visualizing what you would like to experience. In order to tell the new-and-improved story about your physical experience, you must spend time thinking and speaking about the experience you would like to live.

The most powerful thing you can do—the thing that will give you much greater leverage than any action—is to spend time every day visualizing your life as you want it to be. We encourage that you go to a quiet and private environment for 15 minutes every day where you can close your eyes and imagine your body, your environment, your relationships, and your life in ways that please you.

What has been has nothing to do with what will be, and what others experience has nothing to do with your experience . . . but you must find a way to separate yourself from all of that—from the past and from the others—in order to be what you want to be.

What about When One's Desire Overrules One's Belief?

Jerry: People have been running for thousands of years, and no one had been able to cover a mile in four minutes. And then a man named Roger Bannister did it, and once *he* did it, now many others have run the "four-minute mile" as well.

Abraham: When people do not allow the fact that no one else has ever done something to prevent *them* from doing it, they are of great advantage to others, because once they break through and create it, then others can observe and, in time, can come to *believe* or *expect* it—and for that reason, everything that you accomplish is of value to your society.

Your platform for progressive living continues to expand, and life does get better and better for everyone. However, we are wanting to take you beyond the need to see it before you can believe it. We want you to understand that if you believe it, *then* you will see it. Anything that you practice in your mind until the idea begins to feel natural to you must come to physical fruition. The *Law of Attraction* guarantees it.

You will feel enormous liberation when you realize that you do not have to wait for someone else to do something in order to prove that it can be done or before you allow yourself to do it. As you practice new thoughts, reaching for improved emotions, and then see the evidence that the Universe will provide, you will come to know your own true power. *If someone were to tell you that you are experiencing an incurable disease, you could then say with confidence, "I will decide what I will live, for I am the creator of my experience." If your desire is strong enough, it can outweigh your negative beliefs and your recovery will begin.*

It is not so different from the story of the mother whose child is pinned beneath the object that weighs many, many times more than anything she has ever lifted, but in her powerful desire to save her child, she does lift it. Under normal conditions, she could not begin to lift this object, but with such powerful desire, her normal beliefs become temporarily irrelevant. If you said to her, "Do you *believe* you can lift that object?" she would say, "Of course not. I can't even pick up my suitcase when it's full." But *belief* had nothing to do with *this:* Her child was dying, and her *wanting* was to free her child—and so she did.

But What If I Believe in Dangerous Germs?

Jerry: I really do want to be healthy, but I also believe that I might catch some things. And so, whenever I visit people who are in the hospital, I hold my breath as I walk down the corridor to avoid germs.

Abraham: You must have very short visits. (Fun)

Jerry: I do have short visits, and I keep going to a window and trying to get some air. . . . So if I believe that I can avoid the germs by holding my breath, then will that belief keep me from getting sick?

Abraham: In your strange way you are maintaining a vibrational balance. You *want* health, you *believe* that germs could make you sick, you *believe* that your behavior of avoiding the germs is preventing sickness—and so you achieve a balance that works for you. You are, however, going about it the hard way.

If you were really listening to your *Guidance System,* you would not enter an environment where you believe there are germs that could compromise your Well-Being. The dread you feel about going into the hospital is your indicator that you are about to take action before you have achieved vibrational alignment. You could just not go to the hospital, but then you would feel uncomfortable because you know that your sick friend would enjoy a visit from you. So you find a way to visit your friend without feeling dread. And that is what we mean by finding vibrational alignment *before* you take the action of entering the hospital. In time, you can come to *believe* so much in your Well-Being, or your *desire* for Well-Being can become so vivid, that you could be in any environment and not feel a threat to your Well-Being.

When you are in alignment with *who-you-really-are* and you are listening to your powerful *Guidance System,* you would never enter an environment where your Well-Being could be threatened. Unfortunately, many people override their own *Guidance System* for the sake of pleasing others. Two people could enter the hospital as you have described it, one feeling no threat to Well-Being and the other feeling great threat. The first would not get sick; the second one would—not because of the germs that are present in the hospital, but because of the person's vibrational relationship to his or her own sense of Well-Being.

We are not attempting to alter your beliefs, for we do not see your beliefs as inappropriate. It is our desire to make you aware of your own

Emotional Guidance System so that you can achieve the balance of vibration between your desires and your beliefs. Doing the "right" thing means to do that which is in harmony with your intent and with your current beliefs.

Jerry: So there's nothing wrong with taking "the coward's way out"?

Abraham: There are many people who override their own *Guidance System* by trying to please others, and there are many people who will call you "selfish" or "cowardly" when you have the audacity to please yourself rather than them. Often others will call you "selfish" (because you are unwilling to yield to *their* own selfishness) without realizing the hypocrisy of their demand.

Sometimes we are accused of teaching *selfishness,* and we admit that it is true, because if you are not selfish enough to tend to your own vibration and therefore hold yourself in alignment with your Source (with *who you-really-are*), then you have nothing to give to another anyway. When others call you "selfish" or "cowardly," their own vibrations are clearly out of balance, and a modification of *your* behavior will not bring them into balance.

The more you think and speak of your own physical well-being, the more entrenched your own vibrational patterns of wellness will be, and the more the *Law of Attraction* will then surround you with things that enhance and support those beliefs. *The more you tell your own story of Well-Being, the less vulnerable you will feel, and then not only will your point of attraction shift so that different situations will surround you, but you will also feel different about the situations as they come.*

I Am Guided *Toward* What I *Do* Like

Abraham: The only path to the life you desire is through the path of less resistance, or the path of most allowance: allowance of your Connection to your Source, to your *Inner Being,* to *who-you-really-are,* and to all that you desire. And that allowance is indicated to you in the form of good-feeling emotions. If you will let feeling good be your most important priority, then whenever you are having a conversation that is not in harmony with the health you desire, you will feel bad, and so you will be alerted to your resistance . . . and then you can choose a better-feeling thought and you will be right back on track.

Whenever you feel negative emotion, it is your *Guidance System* helping you realize that you are, in this moment, offering resistant thought that is hindering the Stream of Well-Being that would otherwise be reaching you fully. It is as if your *Guidance System* is saying: *Here, you're doing it again; here, you're doing it again; here, you're doing it again. This negative emotion means you are in the process of attracting what you do not want.*

Many people ignore their *Guidance System* by tolerating negative emotion and, in doing so, deny themselves the benefit of Guidance from Broader Perspective. But once life has caused you to identify that you desire something, you will never again be able to look at its opposite or at the lack of it without feeling negative emotion. Once a desire has been born within you, you must look at the desire if you are to feel good. And the reason for that is, *you cannot revert back to less than life has caused you to become.* Once you identify a desire for wellness, or for a specific bodily condition, you will never be able to focus upon the lack of it again without feeling negative emotion.

Whenever you feel negative emotion, just stop whatever it is you are doing or thinking and say, "What is it that I do want?" And then, because you have turned your attention to what you do want, the negative feeling will be replaced by a positive feeling, and the negative attraction will be replaced by positive attraction—and you will be right back on track.

First, I Must Be Willing to Please Myself

Abraham: When you have been on a particular train of thought for a while, it is not easy to abruptly change the direction of your thought, because the *Law of Attraction* is supplying you with thoughts that match your current train of thought. Sometimes while you are in that negative-feeling mode, another who is not in that negative place will not agree with your negative view of your current subject, which only serves to make you want to defend your position all the more. *Trying to defend or justify your opinion only causes you to stay in your resistant state longer. And the reason so many people hold themselves in resistance unnecessarily is because it is more important to them to be "right" rather than to feel good.*

When you meet those who are determined to convince you that they are right, and they try to hold you in a negative conversation in an attempt to convince you, sometimes you are considered "uncaring" or "coldhearted" if you do not hear them and eventually agree with their point of view. But when you forfeit your good feeling (that comes when you choose thoughts that harmonize with your Broader Perspective) to try to please a negative friend who wants to use you as a sounding board, you are paying a very big price for something that will not help him or her either. That uncomfortable knot in your stomach is your *Inner Being* saying, *This behavior, this conversation, isn't in harmony with what you want.* You must be willing to please yourself first or you will often be swept up by the negativity that surrounds you.

Is There an Appropriate Time to Die?

Jerry: Are there any limits of control for our bodily conditions as we approach 100 years of age?

Abraham: Only the limitations caused by your own limited thinking—and all are self-imposed.

Jerry: Is there a time to die, and if so, when is it?

Abraham: There is never an ending to the Consciousness of You, so really there is no "death." But there will come an end to the time that your Consciousness will flow through this particular physical body that you identify as *you.*

It is up to you when you withdraw your focus from this body. If you have learned to focus upon good-feeling subjects, and you continue to find things in this environment that excite you and interest you—there is no limit to the amount of time that you can remain focused in your physical body. But when you focus negatively and chronically diminish your Connection to the Stream of Source Energy, your physical experience is then shortened, for your physical apparatus cannot sustain long-term without Source Energy replenishment. *Your negative emotion is a signal that you are cutting off the Source Energy replenishment. Get happy and live long.*

Are All Deaths a Form of Suicide?

Jerry: So, all deaths are a form of "suicide"?

Abraham: That would be one way of stating it. Since everything that you experience comes about because of the balance of your thought, and no one else can think your thoughts or offer your vibration, then everything that happens in your life experience—including that which you term your physical death—is self-inflicted. *Most do not decide to die—they just do not decide to continue to <u>live.</u>*

Jerry: How do you feel about those who *do* decide to die and commit what we call *suicide?*

Abraham: It makes no difference whether the thought you are thinking is one you have deliberately chosen to focus upon or whether you are merely lazily observing something and therefore thinking the thought—you are still thinking the thought, offering the vibration, and reaping the manifestational result of that thought. So you are always creating your own reality whether you are doing it purposefully or not.

There are those who seek to control your behavior for many different reasons, who even wish to control your behavior regarding your own personal experience, but their frustration level is great because they have no way of controlling others, and every attempt at that control is futile, wasted effort. So, many are uncomfortable with the idea of people deliberately removing themselves from this physical experience by way of "suicide," but we want you to understand that even if you do that, you do not cease to exist, and whether you depart this physical experience by way of deliberate "suicide" or by way of not-deliberate release, the Eternal Being that you are continues to be and looks back on the physical experience you have just left behind only with love and appreciation for the experience.

There are those who are filled with so much hatred as they live in their physical experience that the chronic pinching off from Source and Well-Being is the reason for their death. There are those who simply are no longer finding interesting reasons to focus and remain, who turn their attention to the Non-Physical, and that is the reason for their death. And there are those who have not come to understand Energy or thought or alignment, who desperately want to feel good and can find no way of stopping the chronic pain they have lived for so long that they deliberately choose to reemerge back into the Non-Physical. But in any case, you are Eternal Beings, who, once refocused in the Non-Physical, become whole and renewed and completely aligned with *who-you-really-are.*

Jerry: So, do we each then choose, to some degree, how long we're going to live in each life experience?

Abraham: You come forth intending to live and joyfully expand. When you disregard your *Guidance System,* continuing to find thoughts that disallow your Connection to your Source, you diminish your Connection to your replenishing Source Energy Stream, and without that support, you wither.

A Process to Manage One's Body Weight?

Jerry: What process would you recommend to those wanting to control their body weight?

Abraham: There are so many beliefs upon this subject. So many different methods have been tried, and most Beings who are struggling with the control of body weight have tried many of those methods with little lasting success. And so, their *belief* is that they cannot control their body weight—and so they do not.

We would encourage a visualization of self as you are wanting to be, seeing yourself in that way, thereby attracting it. The ideas and the confirmation from others and all of the circumstances and events that will bring it about easily and quickly for you will come into your experience once you begin to see yourself that way.

When you feel fat, you cannot attract slender. When you feel poor, you cannot attract prosperity. That which you are—the state of being that you *feel*—is the basis from which you attract. That is why "the better it gets, the better it gets; and the worse it gets, the worse it gets."

When you feel very negative about something, do not try to hammer it out and solve it immediately, because your negative attention to it just makes it worse. Distract yourself from the thought until you feel better; and then take another run at it from your positive, fresh perspective.

Jerry: So, is that why people will often go on a "crash diet" and lose massive pounds, and then they'll find themselves gaining it back? Is it because the *desire* was strong, but they didn't have the *belief* and the picture of themselves as this thin person, so they filled the fat picture back in again?

Abraham: They *want* the food; they *believe* that the food will make them fat. And so, as they are giving thought to that which they do *not* want—in *belief,* they create that which they do not want. But that, again, is going about it in the hard way. For the most part, the reason why they lose the weight and then gain it back quickly is that they never gain an image of self as they want it to be. They keep feeling fat. They keep thinking of themselves as that, and that is the image that they hold. . . . Your body will respond to the image of self—always. That is why if you see yourself as healthy—you will be. If you see yourself as slender, or whatever it is you are wanting in terms of muscle or shape or weight—that is what you will be.

Regarding Food, Can I Follow My Bliss?

Abraham: Some have argued that if they do take our advice and follow their bliss—always looking for things that feel good—they would happily eat things that are detrimental to their health or their body weight. People do often choose food to try to fill the void when they are not feeling good. However, if you have been tending to your vibrational balance for a while and you have learned the power of positively directing your thoughts toward an image of your body as you want it to be, then if you believe that eating a particular food is contrary to accomplishing that desire, negative emotion would come forth as guidance. *It is never a good idea to pursue any action that brings forth negative emotion, because the negative emotion means there is an Energy imbalance, and any action that you participate in during negative emotion will always produce negative results.*

Negative emotion does not occur within a person because a particular food is contrary to Well-Being, but because of current contradictory thoughts. Two people could eat identical diets and follow similar exercise programs and get opposite results, which means there is much more to the equation than the consumption of the food and the burning of calories. *Your results are always and only about your alignment of Energy caused by the thoughts you think.*

A good rule of thumb is: "Get happy, then eat. But do not try to eat your way to happiness." As you have come to make your emotional balance your top priority, your relationship with food will change and your impulse toward food will change, but even more important, your response to food will change. Altering _behavior_ about food without tending to your vibration nets minimal results, while altering _thought_ will yield great returns without the necessity of altering the _behavior._

And so, let us say that you have decided that you want to be very slender, but you currently do not see yourself as you want to be. And your belief is: _If I eat this food, I will be fat._ As you have a _desire_ to be slender, but a _belief_ that eating this food will make you fat, you would feel negative emotion if you begin to eat the food. You might call it _guilt, disappointment,_ or _anger_—but whatever it is, _eating the food feels bad because, given the set of beliefs that you hold, and given the desire that you hold, this action is not in harmony. And so, if you are following your bliss, you would find yourself feeling good about eating the things that do harmonize with your beliefs and bad about eating the things that do not. Once a desire has been established within you, it is not possible to offer behavior that you believe contradicts it without feeling negative emotion._

What Are My Beliefs about Food?

Abraham: The beliefs that you hold regarding food are boldly reflected in the experiences you are living:

- If you _believe_ that you can eat most anything and not gain weight, that is your experience.

- If you _believe_ that you gain weight easily, then you do.

- If you _believe_ that certain foods give you an energy boost, they do.

- If you _believe_ that certain foods deflate your energy, they do.

- If you want to be slender, but you _believe_ that a particular diet is not conducive to being slender, and you take the action of eating that diet, you will gain weight.

People often initially balk at our seemingly simplistic analysis of your beliefs about food and how they affect your physical reality, because they believe that their beliefs have come about by observing experience, and it is hard for them to argue with the "factual" evidence that the living of their own life and the observation of others' lives has provided them.

However, observation of results gives you scanty and inadequate information, for unless you are factoring in *desire* and *expectation,* then calculating the action of what has or has not been eaten is irrelevant. You simply cannot leave out the most important ingredient in the recipe of creation and understand the outcome.

People respond differently to the food because the food is not the constant—the thought is. It is the way you are thinking about the food that is making the difference.

Opinions of Others about My Body Are Insignificant

Question: A significant other pointed out to me that I have a little roll along my belt line and it would be good if I worked hard to get rid of it—I could exercise more or eat less or order salads. And because she's a significant other, I took it to heart—and my roll got bigger.

Abraham: The most important thing that we want you to understand is that when you are using the word *other,* always use the word *insignificant* regarding him or her. (Fun)

Of course we understand that people in your life are significant, but you must not let their opinions of you be more important than your own, and anytime anyone influences you to focus upon something that makes you feel bad, you have received negative influence.

We want you to practice your own thoughts so steadily that opinions of others become irrelevant to you. The only freedom you will ever experience comes when you achieve an absence of resistance, which means you will have figured out how to align your chronic thoughts with the thoughts of your own *Inner Being.*

We have never seen anyone achieve that alignment or the feeling of freedom when they are factoring the desires and beliefs of others into the equation. There are just too many moving parts, and it cannot be sorted out.

And so, if someone says to you, "I see something about you that I don't like," we would say, "Look someplace else. What do you think of my nose? Cute little thing, is it not? (Fun) What about this ear over here?" In other words, we would encourage the other to look for positive aspects, and we would be playful and not allow our feelings to be hurt. In fact, we would practice positive thought about our life until we render our feelings unhurtable.

An Example of My "Old" Story about My Body

I'm not happy about the way my body looks. I've been trim and fit at times in my life, but it has never been easy, and those periods never lasted very long. It seems to me that I always had to work irrationally hard to even get close to the way I wanted to look, and then I just couldn't manage to stay there. I'm tired of depriving myself of good things to eat only to end up not looking good anyway. This is hard. I just don't have the kind of metabolism that allows me to eat much of anything that tastes good. It's really not fair. But I don't like being fat either. . . .

An Example of My "New" Story about My Body

My body is a reflection mostly of the thoughts I think. I am happy to understand the power of directing my thoughts, and I am looking forward to seeing physical changes in my body, which reflect my changes in my thinking. I feel good as I anticipate my improved size and shape—and I am confident that those changes are in progress. And, in the meantime, I am generally feeling so good that I am not unhappy with where I currently am. It is fun to think on purpose, and even more fun to see the results of those deliberately chosen thoughts. My body is very responsive to my thoughts. I like knowing that.

There is no right or wrong way to tell your improved story. It can be about your past, present, or future experiences. The only criterion that is important is that you be conscious of your intent to tell a better-feeling, improved version of your story. Telling many good-feeling short stories throughout your day will change your point of attraction. Just remember that the story *you* tell is the basis of *your* life. So tell it the way you want it to be.

PART V

Careers, as Profitable Sources of Pleasure

My First Steps in Career Choice?

Jerry: How would you suggest we know if we've chosen the right career? And how can we be successful at the career we've chosen?

Abraham: What is your definition of *career?*

Jerry: A *career* is like a life's work. An occupation that people could throw themselves into and put the best and the most of themselves into. And, of course, in most cases, people would also want to get a financial return on that.

Abraham: What are you meaning by *life's work?*

Jerry: Some work that people would plan to spend the rest of their lives doing, like a job, profession or business, or a trade. . . .

Abraham: Are you telling us that it is a widespread belief, or accepted desire, of your culture to choose a career and expect to live happily ever after within one topic, forevermore?

Jerry: Well, as long as I can remember, it has been traditionally so. From the time I was very young, people began asking me what I was going to be when I grew up. It is interesting to me now to realize that even when I was a very young child, the adults around me had instilled a sense of urgency in me to choose a career; and I remember watching the milkman delivering the beautiful, delicious milk in glass bottles and thinking as I watched him drive away that that would be my choice for a career. And then I witnessed a policeman actually *making* my mother stop her car by running her off the road, and I was in such admiration of anyone who was able to get my mother to do anything that for a while I decided that I'd be a policeman. Not long after that, a doctor set my broken arm, and I thought I'd like to be a doctor; and then our house caught fire, and the idea of being a fireman seemed like the best idea.

And even after becoming what many would consider to be an adult, I was still observing and considering the multitude of options from my ever-changing perspective. And so, those around me were a bit disappointed that I kept moving from thing to thing rather than settling on one thing for my "life work" or "career."

Abraham: Many people, as they read your childhood story of the events of your life influencing your ideas of what you wanted to be when you grew up, might call your ever-changing ideas childish or unrealistic. But we want to acknowledge: You are always inspired from the events of your life, and when you allow yourself to follow the flow of those inspired ideas, your potential for a joyous experience is much greater than if you were to select your career based on other reasons that people use to justify their choices, such as family tradition or income potential.

It is not surprising that so many have a difficult time deciding what they will do for the rest of their lives, because you are multi-faceted Beings and your dominant intent is to enjoy your absolute basis of freedom and, in your quest for joyful experiences, to experience expansion and growth. In other words, without a real perception of *freedom,* you will never be *joyful;* and without *joy,* you cannot experience true *expansion.* So, childish as it may seem to many, it is natural that your life inspires your next adventure and your next and your next.

We encourage you to decide, as early in life as possible, that your dominant intent and reason for existence is to live happily ever after. That would be a very good career choice: to gravitate toward those activities and to embrace those desires that harmonize with your core intentions, which are freedom and growth—and joy. *Make a "career" of living a happy life rather than trying to find work that will produce enough income that you can do things with your money that will then make you happy. When feeling happy is of paramount importance to you—and what you do "for a living" makes you happy—you have found the best of all combinations.*

You can become very good at feeling good under all conditions, but when you become good at reaching for your vibrational balance first—and then attract circumstances and events to yourself from that happy place—your potential for sustained happiness is much greater.

"What Do You Do for a Living?"

Jerry: There are cultures still today (usually we call them primitive or savage) who seem to live in the moment, without jobs. In other words, when they're hungry, they catch a fish or find fruit in a tree.

Abraham: Will they be reading this? (Fun) [No, they won't.] What is the basic category of people you believe will be reading this?

Jerry: People who believe it is essential to have some sort of an income-producing job.

Abraham: What do you believe is the predominant reason that people believe they should find a career early in life and then pursue it the rest of their lives?

Jerry: Of course, I can't speak for everyone, but it seems to almost be a moral or ethical position that we *should,* or *ought,* to find work that produces money. In other words, it's considered to be inappropriate to receive money without giving something back for it or without being productive in some way.

Abraham: You are right. Most people do feel a need to justify their existence through effort or work, and that is perhaps the reason why the first question that you ask one another upon meeting for the first time is: *What do you do for a living?*

Jerry: For about 40 years, I earned my living by working about an hour and a half a day. And often people would voice a sort of resentment that I could have such an income without putting out more time, which would usually evoke a justification from me as I would then explain how much energy I expended during that 90 minutes, how many years it took me to become good at what I did, or how much driving I had to do to even begin my work. In other words, I always felt a need to justify that I *was* actually paying a fair price for what I was receiving.

Abraham: When you are in vibrational alignment (which means that you are in alignment with the Source within you and that your own desires and beliefs are in balance), you never feel a need to justify to another. Many people attempt to justify their behavior or ideas to others, but it is never a good idea to use opinions of others as the guide that you are seeking alignment with rather than your own *Guidance System.*

Many people early on in your experience attempt to demand your compliance with their rules and opinions, but if you allow what they want to be central to the decisions that you make, you only get further and further out of alignment with *who-you-really-are* and with the intentions that you were born with as well as those that have evolved from the life experience you are living. *You will never experience the deliciousness of feeling free until you release your desire to please others and replace it with your powerful intention to align to <u>who-you-really-are</u> (to your Source) by caring how you feel and choosing good-feeling thoughts that let you know you have found your alignment.*

When you sense that someone is disapproving of you or attacking you, it is a natural response to defend yourself, but that need to defend will quickly subside when you have trained yourself into alignment with your *Inner Being,* because all feelings of vulnerability will have been replaced with a sure-footed sense of *who-you-really-are.*

No matter what choices you make, there will always be someone who does not agree with those choices, but as you find your balance and maintain your alignment, most who are observing you will be more inclined to ask you what your secret to success is rather than criticizing you for being successful. And those who continue to criticize you would find no satisfaction in your justification, no matter how compelling your argument is.

It is not your role to fix the feeling of lack within others; it is your role to keep *yourself* in balance. When you allow your society, or even one other person, to dictate to you what you should want or how you should behave, you will lose your balance, because your sense of freedom—which is core to your very Beingness—is challenged. *When you pay attention to the way you feel and you practice the self-empowering thoughts that align with <u>who-you-really-are,</u> you will offer an example of thriving that will be of tremendous value to those who have the benefit of observing you.*

<u>*You cannot get poor enough to help poor people thrive or sick enough to help sick people get well. You only ever uplift from your position of strength and clarity and alignment.*</u>

The *Law of Attraction,* and Career?

Abraham: What is the primary reason for the desire for a career?

Jerry: I read a study done recently that concluded that what most people are looking for is *prestige.* In other words, if offered the choice of having a higher title or more money, most chose the title.

Abraham: Those who are seeking prestige have replaced their own *Guidance System* with seeking approval from others, and that is a rather unfulfilling way to live because the onlookers you are seeking to please do not sustain long-lasting attention upon you.

That study is very likely accurate because most people do care more about what others think about them than they do about how they personally feel, but there can be no consistency in that form of guidance.

Sometimes people worry that if they selfishly consider what makes them happy above all other things, they will be uncaring and unfair to those around them, but we know that the opposite is true. *When you care about your alignment with Source, which is represented by the way you feel, and you work to maintain your Connection, anyone who is then your object of attention receives benefit from your gaze. You cannot uplift another unless you are connected to the Stream of Well-Being yourself.*

We understand that it can feel very good when others hold you as their object of attention as they are feeling appreciation for you, because they are then doing exactly what we were just explaining to you: In their appreciation of you, they are connected to Source and showering it all over you. But to ask others to always be in alignment with Source and to always hold *you* as their object of attention so that you can be showered with the Well-Being they are providing is not practical, because you cannot control their connection and you will not always be their only object of attention. You do, however, have absolute control over your own Connection to Source, and when your dominant intent is to maintain your Connection while leaving others out of that equation, then you will be free of trying to please others (which you cannot consistently do), and you will be able to maintain a consistent Connection and feeling of Well-Being.

An interesting thing to note is, those who care about how they feel—who consistently hold themselves in an attitude of good-feeling emotions; who are connected to Source and flowing positive thoughts outward toward whatever they are focused upon—are usually seen by others to be *attractive,* and they are often the recipients of much appreciation and approval.

You just cannot get the approval you seek from the place of *needing* it or from the place of the *lack* of it. An office with a wonderful window view or a parking place with your name on it or an impressive title accompanying your name cannot fill the void caused by not being in alignment with *who-you-really-are*. When you achieve that alignment, those things feel less important—but then, interestingly enough, they come anyway.

Filling My Void Through Service?

Jerry: So during my 20 years in a wide variety of positions in the entertainment industry, I really had a lot of fun; it required only a few hours of my time, and I had a lot of adventurous challenges because I had so many new experiences . . . and yet I often told people that I felt like I was walking across the sands of life, but when I looked back, there were no tracks. In other words, I felt that I was bringing my audiences some temporary pleasure, but I wasn't leaving them with anything of permanent value.

Do we all inherently have those drives to uplift others? Do they come from another level of ourselves, or do we pick those intentions up from others around us once we're born into this physical environment?

Abraham: *You are born wanting to be of value, wanting to uplift. And you are born understanding that you have value.* Most of that feeling of lack that you were describing was not about your not being able to provide lasting value to others, but because your thoughts were keeping you away from your own personal alignment. It works like this: When you are in alignment with *who-you-really-are* (with your *Inner Being* or Source), you cannot help but uplift those with whom you come into contact, *and* in that alignment, you do not notice so many others who are not in alignment. *The Law of Attraction does not surround you with dissatisfied people when you are satisfied. And the Law of Attraction does not surround you with satisfied people when you are dissatisfied.*

You simply cannot compensate for your own misalignment by offering more time or energy or action. You cannot find ideas that are effective enough to make up the difference. Your value to those around you hinges upon only one thing: your personal alignment with Source. And the only thing you have to give to another is an example of that alignment—which they may observe, then desire, and then work to achieve. But *you* cannot give it to them.

The entertainment that you provided to your audiences was actually a much bigger gift than you were able to acknowledge at the time, for you were providing distraction from troubling things; and in the absence of your audience members' attention to their problems, they did achieve, in many cases, temporary alignment with Source. But you cannot go with each of them, holding yourself as their only object of attention in order to maintain their good feeling. *Everyone is responsible for the thoughts they think and the things that they choose as their objects of attention.*

All of you have, deep within you, an understanding that you are here as joyous creators, and you are always being called toward that fulfillment, but there is not a long list of requirements that you are expected to accomplish. Your intention was to let your physical environment inspire your never-ending ideas of expansion or desire, and then you intended to align with the Source Energy within you for the achievement of those ideas. In other words, you knew your desires would be born from your participation here, and then, once the desire was alive within you, you could focus your thoughts until you accomplished a feeling of expectation—and then your desire would come to fruition.

The primary role that others around you play in that equation for creation is they provide variety from which your desires are born. *It was not your intention to measure your value against the value of others, but to be inspired to new ideas by the combination of things going on around you. Any comparison to others is only meant to inspire expanded desire. It was never intended as a means to diminish you or to discount your value.*

Your life is not about what you will do after work, on the weekend, or after you retire. Your life is happening now and is really represented by how you are feeling now. If your work feels unpleasant or unfulfilling or hard, it is not because you are standing in the wrong place, but because your perspective is clouded by contradicted thought.

You cannot have a happy ending to a journey that has not been pleasant along the way. The end absolutely does not justify the means.

The means, or the path along the way, always brings about the essence of an identical ending.

Will My Success Uplift Others?

Jerry: My freedom has always been what was most important to me, so I've never been willing to give up much of it for money. I always said that I had very little interest in money because I wasn't willing to give up my freedom for it, but then over time that "leaving no footprints in the sand" feeling made me question if there wasn't really something more to life than just having fun.

Shortly after that awareness, I found the book *Think and Grow Rich,* and even though the idea of *thinking* or of *growing rich* was something that I would have denied having any interest in, the book got my attention and I felt a strong draw toward it. I picked it up and the hair stood up on my body as if I had found something that would have major meaning in my life. The book said: *Make a decision about what you want!* It was a seemingly simple statement, but I felt the power of it in a strange and new way, so for the first time in my life, I consciously started making decisions about what I wanted and writing them down: "I want to be self-employed; I want a business of my own; I want no place of business; I don't want my foot nailed to the floor; I want no employees—I don't want that kind of responsibility. What I want is *freedom.*"

I wanted to be able to control my income. I wanted to be mobile so I could travel or be anywhere that I wanted to be. *I wanted my work to be something where every life I touched I elevated in some way (or just let people be where they were) but that no one would ever be diminished as a result of knowing me.*

People used to laugh when I'd tell them that. They'd say, "Oh, Jerry, you're such a dreamer. There's no such thing as that." And I said, "Well, there has to be. Emerson said, 'You wouldn't have the desire if you didn't have the ability to achieve it.'" And I believed that. And so, I really expected, somewhere along the line, opportunities to show up. . . .

Within about 30 days of my clarifying what I *wanted*, I met a man who showed me a business that I could take to California and start—and it answered everything I was asking for. And so, for the next years of my life, that business really took hold. And again, it fulfilled the essence of everything that I'd written down that I wanted.

I Want Freedom, Growth, and Joy

Jerry: I didn't say it had to be something I was capable of doing or that I had the talent or the ability or the intelligence for; I just said: *This is what I want.*

Can any of us have that? Can any of us have whatever we want once we clarify what it is that we want?

Abraham: Yes. *If this life experience has inspired the desire within you, this life experience has the wherewithal to fulfill it down to the very last detail.*

You had been coming to those decisions about what you wanted over a long period of time because of the life experiences that you had been living. Your decision point of focusing upon those decisions and writing them down in a comprehensive manner caused an emphasizing of your *belief* regarding them. And when your *desires* and *beliefs* come together, *expectation* occurs. And once *expectation* for anything is within you, it then comes quickly into your experience.

Being free was the most important element in the desires that you had held for some time, and when you saw something that you believed would not threaten your desire for freedom but had the potential of bringing income, you then allowed your desire for more income to expand, where previously anything that you perceived as having the potential to dampen your freedom you repelled immediately.

You were all born with a triad of intentions pulsing within you: *freedom, growth,* and *joy. Freedom* is the basis of that which you are because everything that comes to you comes in response to the thoughts you think—and no one has control over the thoughts that you think other than you. When *joy* is your dominant quest so that you gently train your thoughts into alignment with *who-you-really-are,* all resistance subsides, and you then allow the *expansion* or *growth* that your life experience has inspired within you.

I Want My Life to Feel Good

Abraham: *When choosing a career, or when doing the things that your work currently requires, if your dominant intent is to feel joy while you are doing the work, your triad of intentions will come quickly and easily into alignment, because in your accomplishment of feeling good, you come into complete alignment with the broader, Non-Physical aspects of your Being. That alignment then allows the expansion toward all of the things that your life has helped you identify that you want, so your growth becomes swift and satisfying.*

Freedom is the basis of your life experience; it is not something that you have to earn. *Joy* is your objective. *Growth* is the result of all of that. But if you believe that you are unworthy and you set out to prove worthiness through action, you cannot find your balance. Often we explain this perfect triad of intentions of *freedom and growth and joy,* but most physical Beings then turn their attention immediately to the idea of *growth* in their misguided attempt of proving worthiness—worthiness that has never been in question. You have nothing to prove to anyone and nothing to justify. *Your reason for existence needs no justification, for your very existence is jus-tification enough.*

I Create My Own Joyous Career

Abraham: *We would like you to see your "career" as one of creating a joyful life experience. You are not a creator of things or a regurgitator of what someone else has created or a gatherer of stuff. You are a creator, and the subject of your creation is your joyful life experience. That is your mission. That is your quest. That is why you are here.*

Is It Immoral to Get Without Giving?

Jerry: Abraham, would you say that it would be morally or ethically correct for people to never give back? In other words, if they just lived on inherited money or won money, like the lottery, or lived off of welfare or donated money, would you say that would be appropriate for *all* of us?

Abraham: Your question still implies that there is a price to pay for the Well-Being that flows to you, and that some sort of action is required to justify the flowing of the Well-Being. That is not the case. *It is neither necessary nor possible to justify the Well-Being that flows to you, but it is necessary to <u>align</u> with the Well-Being. You cannot focus upon lack of Well-Being and allow Well-Being into your experience.*

Many people focus upon *unwanted* things, with no deliberate attention to the emotional Guidance within them, and then they try to compensate for their lackful thinking with physical action. And because of the misalignment of Energy, they do not get results from their action, so then they try harder by offering more action, but still things do not improve.

Like the air you breathe, abundance in all things is available to you. Your life will simply be as good as you allow it to be.

If you believe that you must work hard for the abundance that comes to you, then it cannot come without hard work. But in so many cases, the harder you work, the worse you feel, and the worse you feel, the more you disallow the results that you wanted to receive from your hard work. It is no wonder so many people are discouraged and do not know which way to turn, for it seems that no matter what they do, they do not thrive.

Appreciation and *love,* and *alignment* to that which is Source, is the ultimate "giving back," so to speak. In your *pain* or *struggle,* you have nothing to give back. Many complain of unfairness or injustice when they see some people receiving greatly but offering seemingly little effort, while others who work very hard often show very little success—but the *Law of Attraction* is always consistently just. <u>*What you are living is always an exact replication of your vibrational*</u>

patterns of thought. Nothing could be more fair than life as you are living it, for as you are thinking, you are vibrating, and as you are vibrating, you are attracting—and so you are always getting back the essence of what you are giving.

Jerry: If we take money out of the equation, so to speak, then if we're not *doing* for the sake of money, what *should* we be doing with our life?

Abraham: What most people *are* doing with most of their lives is offering action to try to compensate for vibrational imbalance. In other words, they think so much of things they *do not want,* and in doing so, they prevent what they *do want* from easily flowing into their experience, and then they try to compensate for the misalignment through action. If you would tend to your vibrational alignment first—by recognizing the value of your emotions and trying to focus upon things that feel good—you would benefit tremendously by that alignment, and wonderful things would flow to you with far less action.

The majority of action that is offered today is offered amidst tremendous vibrational resistance, and that is the reason why so many people have come to believe that life is a struggle. It is also the reason why many, like you, believe that success and freedom are at odds with one another, when, in reality, they are actually synonymous. *It is not necessary to take money out of the equation, but it is necessary that you make your quest for joy be the most dominant part of your equation. When you do that, abundance in all manner will flow to you.*

Welcome to Planet Earth

Abraham: If we were talking to you on your first day of physical experience, we could be of great advantage to you because we would say, "Welcome to planet Earth. There is nothing that you cannot be or do or have. And your work here—your lifetime career—is to seek joy.

"You live in a Universe of absolute freedom. You are so free that every thought you think will attract unto you.

"As you think thoughts that feel good to you, you will be in harmony with *who-you-really-are*. And so, utilize your profound freedom. *Seek joy first, and all of the growth that you could ever imagine will come joyously and abundantly unto you.*"

But this is not the first day of your life experience. In most cases, you are reading this long after you have been convinced that you are not free and that you are unworthy and that you must prove, through your action, that you are worthy of receiving. Many of you are currently involved in careers or work that you do not find pleasing, but you feel that you cannot just walk away because the financial repercussions would cause even greater discomfort than what you are already experiencing. Many others who do not currently have work that is producing income feel the discomfort of having no means of support or promise of future security. But, no matter where you are currently standing, if you will make a decision to look at the positive aspects of where you are right now, you will stop the offering of resistance, which is the only thing holding you apart from what you desire.

You do not have to go back and undo anything or beat up on yourself for what you have not yet accomplished. If you could, in essence, regard this moment as the beginning of your life experience —doing your best to resist the bad-feeling, resistant thoughts of unworthiness or resentment that often surround the subject of money—your financial picture would begin to change right now. You only have to say, *Here I am, on the first day of the rest of my physical life experience. And it is my dominant intent, from this moment forward, to look for reasons to feel good. **I want to feel good. Nothing is more important to me than that I feel good.***

Most Important Is Feeling Good

Abraham: Often there are things in your work environment that are not conducive to feeling good, and often you believe that your only chance of ever really feeling good is to get away from those negative influences. But the idea of quitting and leaving does not feel good either because that could cause a lapse in your income when things are already financially tight, so you continue on, unhappy and feeling trapped.

If you could stand back a little bit and see your career not as work that you are doing in exchange for money but as the expenditure of your life experience in return for your joyful experience, then you would realize that many of the thoughts you think and the words you speak are not in alignment with that quest for joy. If you will say, "Nothing is more important than that I feel good," you will find yourself guiding yourself to different thoughts, words, and behaviors.

The simple exercise of deliberately looking for positive aspects of your current work and the people who work there with you will give you an immediate feeling of relief. And that relief will indicate a shift in your vibration, which means your point of attraction has shifted. Once that occurs, the *Law of Attraction* will cause you to rendezvous with different people and will even cause you to have different experiences with the same people. It is a sort of creating from the inside out, rather than the outside-in, action version that never works. *From your simple but powerful premise of deciding that you want to feel good, things will begin to improve in dramatic ways.*

What Is Holding Back My Career?

Jerry: What would you say to those who are moving toward their first field of employment or are making a career change and are considering things like income or growth potential, product or service demand, and so forth in trying to decide what direction to take?

Abraham: The life you have already lived has caused you to determine the details of the experience you are looking for, and the perfect situation is already lined up for you. Your work right now is not to get out there and find the perfect set of circumstances, but instead to *allow* the unfolding of the circumstances that will lead you right to a position that satisfies the myriad of intentions that you have come to through your life experience. In other words, you never know more clearly what it is that you *do want* than when you are living what you *do not want.*

So, not having enough money causes you to *ask* for more money. An unappreciative employer makes you *ask* for someone who appreciates your talent and willingness. A job that asks very little from you causes you to *desire* something that inspires more clarity and expansion through you. A job that requires a long commute in traffic gives birth to a *desire* for work that is closer to where you live . . . and so on. *We would like to convey to anyone looking for a change in their work environment: It is already queued up for you in a sort of Vibrational Escrow. Your work is to align with what your past and current experiences have helped you identify that you want.*

It may sound strange, but the fastest way to an improved work environment is to look for things in your current environment that make you feel good. Most people do exactly the opposite by pointing out the flaws in where they stand in an effort to justify an improved environment. But since the *Law of Attraction* always gives you more of whatever you are giving your attention to, if your attention is upon unwanted things, then more unwanted things are on the way as well. *When you leave one situation because of the unwanted things that are present, you find the essence of the same unwanted things in your next environment as well.*

Think and speak of what you *do* want.

Make lists of things that are pleasant about where you are.

Think excitedly about the improvements that are on the way to you.

De-emphasize what you do not like.

Emphasize what you do like.

Observe the Universe's response to your improved vibration.

I'll Seek Reasons to Feel Good

Jerry: So, in other words, unless people now focus on what they *do* want and get their focus off of what they *don't* want in their current or previous position, they'll just continue to—in some form—re-create a negative situation?

Abraham: That is absolutely correct. *No matter how justified you are in your negative emotion, you are still messing up your future.*

Most of you have given enough thought to what you want to keep you happily busy for 10 or 20 lifetimes, but your manifestations cannot get to you because your door is closed. And the reason that your door is closed is because you are so busy complaining about *what-is* or busy defending where you now stand. . . . *Look for reasons to feel good. And in your joy, you open the door. And as you open your door, all of these things that you have said "I want" can then flow in. And it is our expectation that, under those conditions, you would live happily ever after—which, after all, is that which you have truly intended as you have come forth into this career of physical life experience.*

Do I *Want* to, or Do I *Have* to?

Jerry: Through my early years while we lived on a series of 40-acre farms in Oklahoma, Missouri, and Arkansas, I did many different things to earn money, all of them very hard work and none of them fun. From picking berries; to raising and selling chickens; to planting, harvesting, and selling tomatoes; to chopping and selling firewood, I earned quite a bit of money (for those times), but I didn't enjoy my work at all. Then, during my high school years in New Orleans, I worked at another series of non-fun jobs as a roofer, a sheet-metal mechanic, and an elevator operator. The first job I had that was any fun at all was being a lifeguard at Pontchartrain Beach.

I guess I was like most others around me, and it didn't occur to me that fun and earning money could coincide. During the time I was doing all of that not-fun, very hard work, I was doing fun things *after* work. I got together with other kids in the park at night and played my guitar, and I sang at church and in the choir with the New Orleans Opera. I led a Cub Scout group, performed acrobatics, and volunteered as a teacher of gymnastics and dance. I did many wonderful, fun things, but I didn't earn money from any of them.

However, once I became an adult, I never again worked very long at anything I didn't enjoy. Instead, I became self-employed, and those things I'd been doing free for fun, I just kept doing—but then I started receiving money in return for performing them.

I hadn't been training for, or planning for, a career in music or singing or dancing or acrobatics—but then the sheet-metal workers' union called a strike, and while I was out of work, a man at the YMCA gym asked me to join "El Gran Circo de Santos y Artigas" in Cuba as an aerial bar performer (*artista*). And so I didn't go in the "secure" direction in roofing and sheet metal that my father wanted me to plan for. (It paid a steady wage, and I was trained for it and was very good at it even though I disliked so much about it.) But as a result of the *unwanted* union strike, I turned easily in the direction of what then became a truly joyous life of adventure and earnings. I began as an acrobat with that Cuban circus and then stayed in show business, in one aspect or another, for over 20 years.

Abraham: Hear how the details of your life clearly demonstrate the things we have been offering here. Do you see how those early years of working so hard at things you did not enjoy helped you to not only identify what you did not want, but also helped you to determine what you did prefer? And even though you were working as a teenager still at things you did not enjoy doing, you were spending a great deal of your time—every spare minute, really—doing things that you really *did* like very much to do. So the two parts of your equation for joyful creation were in place: The hard work caused you to *ask;* your time playing music and doing the gymnastics and such that you loved put you in a chronic place of *allowing;* and then, through the path of least resistance, the Universe delivered to you a viable path to get the freedom, growth, and joy that you wanted.

Because of the intense unpleasantness of those early years of very hard work, you were one of the few who was strange enough or weird enough or different enough to allow yourself to seek your bliss. And that led to many things that you had come to desire.

Most people feel a stark difference between the things that they *want* to do and the things that they believe they *have* to do. And most have put anything that earns money in the category of *the things that I have to do.* That is why the money often comes so hard, and that is why there is usually not enough.

If you are wise enough to follow the trail of good-feeling thoughts, you will discover that that blissful path will lead you to all things you desire. By deliberately looking for positive aspects along your way, you will come into vibrational alignment with who-you-really-are and with the things you really want, and once you do that, the Universe must deliver to you a viable means to achieve your desires.

What If My Pleasure Attracts Money?

Jerry: For example, Esther and I had no intention of receiving income from our work with you, Abraham. We were really enjoying learning from you, and we were thrilled by the positive results we were personally receiving as we applied what we were learning, but it was never our intention for our work with you to become a business. It was an enlightening experience of just plain fun (and it still is fun), but now it has expanded dramatically into a worldwide enterprise.

Abraham: So, are you saying that as your life experience expanded, your ideas and desires expanded, also? And even though in the beginning you were not able to see or describe the details of *how* things would unfold . . . because it was fun and because you felt good, this became a powerful avenue to fulfill desires and goals that had been in place long before you met us or began this work?

Jerry: Yes. My original intention in visiting with you was to learn a more effective way to help others become more financially successful. And, also, I wanted to learn how to live our lives more in harmony with the natural *Laws of the Universe.*

I Want My Work to Feel Free

Jerry: So, most of what you might call my *careers* through the years almost never began as a means to earn money. They've mostly been things that I just enjoyed doing, which ended up earning money.

Abraham: Well, that truly is the secret to the success that you have enjoyed for so many years. Because you determined early on that feeling good was what mattered most to you, you managed to find a variety of interesting ways to maintain that intention, not realizing at the time that *the secret to all success is keeping yourself happy.*

Many of you have been taught that your own happiness is a selfish and inappropriate quest, and that your real objectives should revolve around commitment and responsibility and struggle and sacrifice . . . but we want you to understand that you can be committed and responsible and an uplifter—*and* happy. In fact, unless you do find a way of connecting to your true happiness, all of those other quests are usually just empty, hollow words not backed up by any true value. *You only ever uplift from your position of connection and strength.*

People often say, "I don't want to work," meaning: "I don't want to go someplace where I have to do unwanted things to earn money." And when we ask why, they say, "Because I want to be free." But it is not freedom from action that you are seeking, because action can be fun. And it is not freedom from money that you want, because money and freedom are synonymous. *You are seeking freedom from negativity, from resistance, from the disallowance of who-you-really-are, and from the disallowance of the abundance that is your birthright. You are seeking freedom from lack.*

What Are Its Positive Aspects?

Abraham: *Whenever you feel negative emotion, that is your Emotional Guidance System giving you an indication that you are, in that* *moment, looking at negative aspects of something, and in doing so, you are depriving yourself of something wanted.*

If you will set an intention to look for positive aspects in whatever you are giving your attention to, you will begin to immediately see the evidence of the lifting of patterns of resistance as the Universe is then allowed, by your shift in vibration, to deliver your long-wanted desires to you.

People often move from job to job, profession to profession, employer to employer, only to find the next place no better than the last—and the reason for that is, they take themselves everywhere they go. When you go to a new place and you continue to complain about what was wrong with your last position in order to explain why you came to the new position, the same vibrational mix of resistance goes with you and continues to prevent the things you want from coming to you.

The best way to accomplish an improved work environment is to focus upon the best things about where you currently are until you flood your own vibrational patterns of thought with *appreciation,* and in that changed vibration, you can then allow the new-and-improved conditions and circumstances to come into your experience.

Some worry that if they follow our encouragement to look for good things about where they are, it will only hold them longer in an unwanted place, but the opposite is really true: *In your state of appreciation, you lift all self-imposed limitations (and all limitations are self-imposed) and you free yourself for the receiving of wonderful things.*

Jerry: Abraham, what is the role of *appreciation* in the creation equation? And how does a condition of appreciation equate to what's called the attitude of gratitude? From Napoleon Hill's book *Think and Grow Rich,* I learned to decide what I wanted and then to focus on it (or think about it) until it came into being. In other words, I set goals and timetables for their achievement. But then after meeting you, I became aware that most of what I would describe as the most wonderful things that came into my life weren't so much things that I had specified that I *wanted* (although much of that came to pass, also). What actually manifested was the essence of something that I had greatly *appreciated.*

In other words, I knew Esther for years before we came together. And I never *wanted* her through those years, but I did greatly *appreciate* so many aspects of who she was . . . and then she (and all of her delightful aspects) came completely into my life. And look at what a magnificent difference she has made in the joyous aspects of my life.

Also, I read the *Seth* books over and over and never *desired* to have a "Seth" in my life. But I greatly *appreciated* the teaching of that "Non-Physical Entity" named Seth, as well as Jane Roberts and Robert Butts, who facilitated that experience. And now, here you are, not "Seth" per se, but you bring with you the essence of everything that I *appreciated* so much about Jane and Rob and Seth's phenomenal metaphysical experiences.

Over 40 years ago, I was visiting a family near San Francisco who earned their money from a very basic, almost primitive, mail-order lapidary business that they conducted from their home. I never, ever said that I *wanted* that business, but in my *appreciation,* I told thousands of people the story of that experience. And then one day (about 20 years ago) as I was at the post office picking up orders for some *Teachings of Abraham* recordings, I realized that I was now experiencing the essence of that mail-order business that I had so much *appreciated*—and now look at how many millions of people have been positively touched as a result of the business aspects of disseminating this philosophy!

I could list many more, but I'll add one more scenario: Esther and I, when we first moved to San Antonio, Texas, found a small temporary rental house where we could enjoy a vegetable garden, laying hens, a milk goat, and our own water well. . . . We used to take our walks by crossing the road in front of the house and then walking across a small airplane landing strip into a grove of large cedar and live-oak trees. Even in the heat of the summer, we were able to enjoy our walks by following the deer trails that tunneled through the dense growth of trees.

One day we discovered that one of the deer trails opened into a tiny "meadow" hidden among the oaks. It was so beautiful! The grass and flowers and general atmosphere would be best described as "enchanting." Esther and I loved that good-feeling spot in the woods, and we returned there many times. We conjured scenarios of how this seemingly ancient, seemingly natural clearing could have come about and who might have discovered and enjoyed it before us. We questioned why it was so inexplicably pleasing to us—and we *appreciated* it greatly! We *never* said that we *wanted* that piece of land—we purely *appreciated* it.

And then about five or six years later, a stranger called us and said he had heard that we were looking for land to build our office complex on . . . and the seven acres that he offered us contained that small hidden meadow. And now our office sits exactly on that beautiful, enchanting spot. That 7 acres became part of 20 . . . and then one day I was *appreciating* the beautiful oak trees on our neighbor's prime 20 acres, and to make a long, delightful story relatively short—that little meadow has now evolved to 40 prime acres with Interstate 10 frontage . . . with a plane hangar, a helicopter pad, and a stable (we don't have a plane or horses). *And it all evolved from our appreciation of that small meadow in the woods.*

Abraham, would you please respond to my perspective regarding the emotion of *appreciation?*

Abraham: The vibration of true love, that feeling of being in love, that feeling that you have sometimes when you see someone and you feel like you are moving through one another. The feeling that you have when you are looking at the innocence of a child and feeling the beauty and power of that child. *Love* and *appreciation* are identical vibrations.

Appreciation is the vibration of alignment with <u>who-you-are.</u> It is the absence of resistance. It is the absence of doubt and fear. It is the absence of self-denial or hatred toward others. Appreciation is the absence of everything that feels bad and the presence of everything that feels good. When you focus upon what you want—when you tell the story of how you want your life to be—you will come closer and closer to the vicinity of appreciation, and when you reach it, it will pull you toward all things that you consider to be good in a very powerful way.

Conversely, let us talk about the difference between, let us say, *gratitude* and *appreciation.* Many people use the words interchangeably, but we do not feel the same vibrational essence in them at all, because when you feel gratitude, often you are looking at a struggle that you have overcome. In other words, you are happy that you are still not in the struggle, but there is still some of that "struggle" vibration present. In other words, the difference between *inspiration,* which is being called to *who-you-are,* and *motivation,* which is trying to make yourself go somewhere, is a similar difference.

Appreciation is that tuned-in, tapped-in, turned-on feeling. Appreciation is vibrational alignment with "who I have become." The state of appreciation is "me being in sync with the whole of that which I am."

Being in the state of appreciation is seeing whatever you are looking at through the eyes of Source. And when you are in that state of appreciation, you could walk down a crowded street with all kinds of things that a lot of other people would find reason to criticize or worry about, and you would not have access to them because your vibration of appreciation is picking out for you things of a different vibrational nature.

A state of appreciation is a state of Godliness. A state of appreciation is being *who-you-really-are.* A state of appreciation is who you were the day you were born and who you will be the moment you die, and it would be (if we were standing in your physical shoes) our quest in every moment.

Joseph Campbell used the word *bliss,* and we think it is equal: "Follow your bliss." But sometimes, you cannot get a whiff of bliss from where you are. So we say, if you are in despair, follow your revenge; it is *downstream.* If you are in revenge, follow your hatred; it is *downstream.* If you are in hatred, follow your anger; it is *downstream.* If you are in anger, follow your frustration; it is *downstream.* If you are in frustration, follow your hope; it is *downstream.* If you are in hope, now you are in the vicinity of appreciation.

Once you get into the vibration of hope, now begin making lists of things that you feel good about, and fill your notebooks full of them. Make lists of positive aspects. Make lists of things you love. Go to the restaurant and look for your favorite things, and never complain about anything. Look for the thing that you like the best . . . even if there was only one thing in all of it that you like, give it your undivided attention—and use it as your excuse to be *who-you-are.*

And as you use those things that shine bright and make you feel good as your excuse to give your attention and be *who-you-are,* you will tune to *who-you-are,* and the whole world will begin to transform before your eyes. *It is not your job to transform the world for others—but it is your job to transform it for you.* A state of *appreciation* is pure Connection to Source where there is no perception of lack.

My Time at Work Is Perceptual

Abraham: In the same way that many people are focused upon a shortage of *money,* there are also many who are focused upon a shortage of *time,* and often these two lackful subjects are intertwined to negatively impact one another. Usually the reason for this detrimental coupling of lackful subjects is the feeling that there just is not enough time to do what is necessary to achieve success.

The primary reason that people feel a shortage of time is because they are trying to get too much leverage out of their action. If you are unaware of the power of alignment and are making little or no effort at finding your personal alignment—if you are overwhelmed or angry or resentful or ornery, and from those emotional perspectives, you are then offering your action to try to accomplish things—you are very likely experiencing a severe shortage of time.

There simply is not enough action in the world to compensate for the misalignment of Energy, but when you care about how you feel and you tend to your vibrational balance first, then you experience what feels like a cooperative Universe that seems to open doors for you everywhere. The physical *effort* required of someone who is in alignment is a fraction of that required to someone who is not. The *results* experienced by someone who is in alignment are tremendous in comparison with the results experienced by someone who is not.

If you are feeling a shortage of time or money, your best effort would be to focus upon better-feeling thoughts, to make long lists of positive aspects, to look for reasons to feel good, and to do more things that make you feel good when you do them. Taking the time to feel better, to find positive aspects, to align with who-you-really-are, will net you tremendous results and help you balance your time much more effectively.

Shortage of time is not your problem. Shortage of money is not your problem. Shortage of Connection to the Energy that creates worlds is what is at the heart of all sensations of shortage that you are experiencing. Those voids or shortages can be filled with only one thing: Connection to Source and alignment with *who-you-really-are.*

Your time is a perceptual thing, and even though the clock is ticking the same for everyone, your alignment affects your perception, as well as the results that you allow. When you set time aside to envision your life as you want it to be, you access a power that is unavailable to you when you focus upon the problems of your life.

As you observe the enormous differences in the effort that people apply and the results they achieve, you have to conclude that there is more to the equation of achieving than action alone. The difference is that some receive the benefit of the leverage of alignment because of the thoughts they think—while others disallow that leverage because of the thoughts they think.

Imagine yourself running one mile, and in this mile there are 2,000 doors to move through. Imagine coming to each door and then having to personally open it before you can run through it. Now imagine running the mile, and as you approach each door, the door is opened for you, so you are able to continue the pace, slowing not at all upon approaching each door. *When you are in alignment with the Energy that creates worlds, you no longer have to stop and open the doors. Your Energy alignment allows things to line up for you, and the action that you offer is the way you enjoy the benefit of the alignment you have accomplished.*

Should I Try to Work Harder?

Abraham: You are a powerful creator who came into this Leading Edge environment understanding that you would create through the power of your thought by deliberately directing your focus toward things that you want. You did not intend to rely on your action for that creation.

It may take some time to adjust to the understanding that you are creating through your thoughts, not through your action—but we cannot overstate the value of thinking and speaking of things as you would like them to be rather than as they are. *Once you not only understand the power of your thought, but you deliberately direct this powerful tool in the direction of things that you desire, then you will discover that the action part of your life is the way you enjoy what you have created through your thought.*

When you achieve vibrational alignment (which means your thoughts are pleasing as you think them) and you feel an inspiration to act, you have accomplished the best of both worlds. Your action feels effortless when you are tuned in to the vibrational frequency of Source, and then you feel an inspiration to offer action. Those outcomes are always pleasing. But action taken without tending to vibrational alignment first is hardworking, inefficient action that, over time, wears you down.

Most are so busy dealing with that which is immediate that they do not have time to tend to that which is important. Many tell us that they are so busy making their money that they do not have time to enjoy it . . . for when you rely on your action to create, often you are too tired to enjoy your creation.

Question: My work is an adventure, and I really do enjoy it. But when I tie money and earnings to my work, I can feel a tension that then takes the joy out of it. Do they not go well together?

Abraham: This is a common story that we hear from creative people who are involved in music or art that they love, but when they decide to make this thing they love the primary source of their income, not only do they often struggle in making enough money, but their previous joy is diminished as well.

Most people have a rather negative attitude about money, simply because most people speak more often of what they cannot afford or the lack of the money they desire than they speak of the *benefit* of money. Also, most people spend much more time thinking about what is currently happening in their experience rather than what they would prefer to happen, and so without meaning to, most people are thinking rather lackfully about money.

So then, when you couple an idea of something that you enjoy—your adventure, your music, your art—with something that you have felt strong lack about for a long time (money), the balance of your thought tips toward the dominant feeling.

As you begin spending more time visualizing what you desire and less time observing *what-is,* and as you then practice your more positive, better-feeling story, in time your *adventure* will become the dominant vibration within you, and then as you couple your adventure with your means of earning, the two will blend perfectly and enhance each other.

There is no better way to earn money than to do the things that you love to do. Money can flow into your experience through endless avenues. It is not the choice of the craft that limits the money that flows—but only your attitude toward money.

That is why so many niche markets are continually opening, with people becoming very wealthy from ideas that only recently were not viable markets at all. You are the creator of your own reality, and you are the creator of your own markets of enterprise and your own flow of money.

You cannot accurately define some activities as <u>hard</u> and others as <u>easy,</u> because all things that are in harmony with what you are wanting are easy and flowing, while all things that are not in harmony with what you are wanting are harder and are more resistant.

Anytime what you are doing feels like a struggle, you must understand that your contradictory thought is introducing resistance into the equation. Resistance is caused by thinking about what you do not want, and that is what makes you tired.

An Example of My "Old" Story about My Career

I've always worked hard in every job I've had, but I've never really been appreciated. It seems to me that employers always take advantage of me, getting everything from me that they can and giving as little in return as they can get away with. I'm tired of working so hard for so little. I'm going to start holding back, too—no point in my knocking myself out when no one else notices. Many of the people around me at work know less than I know, work less than I work, and make more money than I make. That's just not right.

An Example of My "New" Story about My Career

I know that I will not always be right here in this place doing this same work. I like understanding that things are always evolving, and it is fun to anticipate where I am headed.

While there are many things that could be better where I am, it is not really a problem because "where I am" is constantly changing to something better. I like knowing that as I look for the best things around me where I am, those things become more prevalent in my experience.

It is fun to know that things are always working out for me, and I watch for the evidence of that . . . and I see more evidence of that every day.

There is no right or wrong way to tell your improved story. It can be about your past, present, or future experiences. The only criterion that is important is that you be conscious of your intent to tell a better-feeling, improved version of your story. By telling many good-feeling short stories throughout your day, you will change your point of attraction.

Time to Tell a New Story

My old story is about . . .

. . . things that have gone wrong.
. . . things that aren't the way I want them to be or think
    they should be.
. . . others who have let me down.
. . . others who have not been truthful with me.
. . . not enough money.
. . . not enough time.
. . . how things usually are.
. . . how things have been all my life.
. . . how things have been lately.
. . . injustices that I see in the world.
. . . others who just don't understand.
. . . others who don't make an effort.
. . . others who are capable but who don't apply themselves.
. . . dissatisfaction with my appearance.
. . . worry about my body's health.
. . . people who take advantage of others.
. . . people who want to control me.

My new story is about . . .

. . . the positive aspects of my current subject of attention.
. . . the way I really want things to be.
. . . how well things are going.
. . . how the *Law of Attraction* is the true manager of all
    things.
. . . abundance that flows abundantly.
. . . how time is perceptual and endless.
. . . the best things I see.
. . . my favorite memories.
. . . the obvious expansion of my life.
. . . the amazing or interesting or wonderful aspects of my
    world.

. . . the incredible variety that surrounds me.

. . . the willingness and effectiveness of so many.

. . . the power of my own thoughts.

. . . the positive aspects of my own body.

. . . the stable basis of my physical body.

. . . how we all create our own reality.

. . . my absolute freedom and my joyous awareness of it.

Each and every component that makes up your life experience is drawn to you by the powerful *Law of Attraction*'s response to the thoughts you think and the story you tell about your life. Your money and financial assets; your body's state of wellness, clarity, flexibility, size, and shape; your work environment, how you are treated, work satisfaction, and rewards—indeed, the very happiness of your life experience in general—is all happening because of the story that you tell. *If you will let your dominant intention be to revise and improve the content of the story you tell every day of your life, it is our absolute promise to you that your life will become that ever-improving story. For by the powerful Law of Attraction, it must be!*

❧ ❧ ❧ ❧ ❧ ❧

Transcript
of Abraham Live:
A *Law of Attraction*
Workshop

(This *Law of Attraction* workshop was recorded in Boston, Massachusetts, on Saturday, September 29, 2007; and this live session is included on a CD in this book for your listening pleasure. [It has been edited slightly for clarity in these pages.] For additional tapes, CDs, books, videos, catalogs, and DVDs, or to reserve your space at an Abraham-Hicks *Law of Attraction* Workshop, please call [830] 755-2299; or write to Abraham-Hicks Publications at P.O. Box 690070, San Antonio, Texas 78269. Also, for an immediate overview of our works, visit our interactive Website at: **www. abraham-hicks.com**.)

Is This a Vibrational Match?

Good morning. We are extremely pleased that you are here. It is good to come together for the purpose of co-creating, do you agree? You are knowing what you are wanting? Really? Well, we believe that you believe that you do, to some extent. In other words, knowing what you *don't* want helps you to know what you *do* want, doesn't it?

So, let us put it in another way: Do you believe that you are a Vibrational Match to your desires? Really? Well, let us tell you how you can tell if you are a Vibrational Match to your desires: You're living them. When you are a Vibrational Match to what you want—you're living it. When you're a Vibrational Match to the *dollars* that your life has helped you to discern that you prefer—you have them, you are spending them, you have access to them . . . they are flowing in and out and in and out and in and out of your experience. When you're a Vibrational Match to the *relationship* that your lifetime has caused you to hone—you're living it.

So, it was a trick question (don't feel bad) because most of our physical friends really think that when we ask, *Do you know what you want?* that we're talking about those things that are still on the not-yet-manifested side of the scale. In other words, *I still want it.*

Someone said to us one day—when we were trying to get her to focus upon positive things, and we sort of laid out a list of positive things that she might think about—"Oh, Abraham, I don't want those; I've already got those." And what she really meant was: "The things that I want are the things that have not yet happened."

We want to help you to realize that if you're thinking about things that you want from the standpoint that they have not yet come to fruition (that they are still missing in your experience; that you are still living the absence of them; and, even more important, if you are feeling any negative emotion around them such as frustration about how long it's taking or disappointment that it has eluded you while someone else is living it), then that is really a strong indicator of the vibrational frequency that you are offering on a regular basis (you might even call it a chronic vibrational offering, which is what a *belief* is); then you're holding it in a sort of suspended position where the distance between where you are and where it is, is not closing. In other words, that's why so many people live for so long in the same situation.

Have you known people like that—that have a bad relationship and they complain about it every time you get together with them, and the relationship then ends because they finally have had enough and they close that door . . . and then, first thing you know, they're telling you about a new relationship, and the next thing you know, they're complaining about that one, too?

And if you have any kind of memory at all, if you're paying attention to them at all (or maybe it's *you* we are talking about), then you have to be noticing that different faces, different places are moving through their experience, but not very much is changing. It's like they keep marrying the same person over and over again. [Fun] They keep dating the same person over and over again. They keep moving into the same neighborhood with the same neighbors and living in the same houses with the same problems.

Jerry says to Esther, "You've still got that floor thing going on, don't you?" as project after project has a problem with the floor.

And Esther will say, "I care about floors."

And Jerry will say, "That's obvious. If you weren't thinking about them at all, we could get a *perfect* floor." [Fun]

You have these patterns of thought, and the *Law of Attraction* is helping you to sustain the pattern of belief that you have. (A belief is just a thought you keep thinking.) And so, early on in your experience, by your exposure to life, you began developing some patterns of thought. Sometimes they were carefully taught to you by others. Sometimes it came because of something that you observed and then talked about and then remembered—and then attracted again . . . and then talked about it and then remembered—and then attracted again.

In other words, life is very interesting here, isn't it? You can't talk about anything for very long before it begins to replicate itself in your life experience. And it's what makes you develop your patterns of what you call *truths*. You say, "At first I wasn't sure, and then I pondered it for a while. And once I gave it my attention, I began seeing evidence of it everywhere. And now I *believe* it. And now that I believe it, it's manifesting in my experience."

And we say, that's really wonderful, isn't it? . . . If it's stuff you want. But if you are repeating patterns of thought about things you do *not* want—and in your environment, oh, you are very, very good at that—you have this sort of Mass Consciousness theory that goes like this: If we don't beat the drum of our history, we are sure to repeat it again.

And we say, the contrary is true: The more you beat the drum of anything, the more you activate the essence of it in your vibration. The more it is activated in your vibration, then the more the *Law of Attraction* is matching you up with things like it. And the more the *Law of Attraction* is matching you up with things like it, the more you observe it. And the more you observe it, the more you talk about it. The more you talk about it and observe it, the more you beat the drum of it or offer the vibration of it.

The more you offer the vibration of it, the more Law of Attraction matches you up with it. The more Law of Attraction matches you up with it, the more you're living it, the more you're talking about it, the more you're beating the drum of it, the more you're offering the vibration of it. . . . The more you're offering the vibration of it, the more the Law of Attraction lines you up with it. The more the Law of Attraction lines you up with it, the more you notice it. The more you notice it, the more you talk about it. The more you talk about it, the more you offer it vibrationally. The more you offer it vibrationally, the more the Law of Attraction lines you up with it. The more the Law of Attraction lines. . . . We could go on. [Fun] Your life experience is showing you that: You just cannot keep telling the same story without continuing to live the same circumstances.

And so, this gathering—we're calling it: *The Art of Telling a Different Story.* The art of telling the story the way life has helped you carve it out incrementally, but telling the story with your words, with your observations, with your expectations, with your vibration. Then, when the *Law of Attraction* is responding to your *deliberate* offering of thought, now you're *getting* what you *want*, not just what you are *observing*.

You're Vibrating Source Energy

It is so interesting to listen to so many of our human friends telling us that the reason that they are talking about something is because it is "true." And we say, that really is a poor excuse, because there are so many things that are true. *True* only means somebody gave their attention to it, offered a vibration about it, and the *Law of Attraction* gave it to them. As the *Law of Attraction* gave it to them, they observed it. As they observed it, they offered a vibra— oh, we've told you that story. [Fun] The only reason that anything is true in anyone's experience is because, somehow, some way, they've begun offering a vibration about it.

You are the creator of your own life experience, whether you know that you are or not—so you might as well do it *deliberately.* You can't turn your vibration off. You're always radiating a vibration, and the *Law of Attraction* is always responding to your vibration, so you may as well offer it on purpose.

Many say, "Well, I *am.* I am offering it on purpose, because I am so aware of the things that I do *not* want, and I am stubbornly making sure that those unwanted things do not come into my experience. And let me tell you the list of things I *don't* want so that you can be sure that none of these unwanted things ever come to me. It's a long list. I've been gathering it for a lifetime, and I'm really good at it. [Fun] And I can give it to you cleverly. I can make you laugh as I repeat the problems of my life experience to you. I've been entertaining people with this for years. [Fun] And so, just sit back and enjoy my explanation of why my life is not going the way I want it to. And once I have repeated this story again (I've done it thousands of times)—once I have repeated this story again—then I'm going to ask the *Law of Attraction* to hear me clearly and give me exactly the opposite of it."

And we say, the *Law of Attraction* is such a fair friend. The *Law of Attraction* will always replicate your vibration. And we want you to remember that your vibration—your vibrational balance, your vibrational countenance, your point of attraction, what's being matched up with you—is always known best by you by the way you *feel.*

The way you feel is your indication of your balance of vibration. Now, here's why: You are Source Energy in a physical body, and many of you know that. You've been talking about *God;* you've been talking about *Source;* you've been talking about *Souls;* you've been talking about *heaven* and *angels;* you've been trying to get your thoughts wrapped around the idea of the Eternalness of *who-you-are.* Many of you have believed, long before you came to know us, that there was life before this body (and you are hoping that there will be life after this body). And we want to say to you that most of what you think about all of that is really screwy. [Fun]

We want you to understand that you are an Eternal Being. But you're not dead or alive. You're not an angel and then a mortal. You're not there with Source and then here without Source. *You are always Source Energy; you are vibration mostly, and this physical Being that you know as you and all of the physical trappings that surround you are interpretations of vibration that you have fashioned into this wonderful world that you are living.*

You are here focused in your physical bodies on the Leading Edge of thought. And it is magnificent that you are here. But we want so much for you to realize that *all* of you didn't come forth into this physical body. And we don't mean *all* of you in terms of the masses; we mean *all* of you in terms of *You*. The larger part of you will always be stable, Non-Physical, Pure, Positive, God Force, Source, Love Energy. That's *who-you-are,* and part of that Consciousness is projected here in this physical body.

Just like the whole of *who-you-are* in this physical body is not attending this workshop here today—you're still a mother or a father or a sister or a brother or a bowler or an accountant—there are many aspects to your life that are not taking place right here and now while you're focused here with us. So, we want you to understand that, in the greater sense of the word, the larger part of you is Non-Physically focused and taking in the benefit that you are providing by being here in this physical body.

All Was Vibrational Thought

Do you get that you were Source Energy before you were in this body? And do you follow our thought that that Source Energy part of you still resides in Non-Physical? Sort of like the electricity passes through the walls of your building, you plug your toaster in, and you toast toast. And someone would say, "Well, then why doesn't the electricity *be* the toaster?" And we say, because the electricity is the electricity; the toaster is the toaster. The Source Energy part of you is the Source Energy part of you—the physical part of you is the "toaster." But it all works together because, here in your physical expression, you are exploring. You are out here on the Leading Edge. You are arriving at the new Leading Edge conclusion, to which the Source within you is then saying, "We agree, and we have become the vibrational equivalent of it."

You'd have to stand back pretty far in order to know what we know about the creation of things—about the creation of your planet, about the creation of what you call *life on planet Earth*—but we want you to know that everything that is what you call manifestation (knock-on-wood, physical stuff that you can discern with your physical senses) . . . every bit of it was vibration first. *Everything is a thought first, and then a vibrational thought that is thought upon longer, until, in time, with enough attention to it, it takes shape and form.*

You are so sure of the reality that you live as you are discerning and agreeing with each other about so many of the conditions of your environment. You have divined your time-space reality in ways that you agree. You say, "We see this room, and we measure it and we come to agreement about how big it is. We know about square footage. We know about measurements. We know about distance. We agree on colors, most of us. We are in agreement with so many things because we are using our physical senses to decipher vibration."

And what we want you to try to get your thoughts around (we know it isn't easy, because the reality of your physical environment feels so permanent and so solid, so static and so real) is: *It is all vibration in motion, and it is all being interpreted by you who are perceiving it.*

What you see with your eyes is only a vibrational interpretation. What you hear with your ears—even what you smell and taste, and feel with your fingertips—these are vibrational interpretations. And because you have been doing it for such a long time and you've been in agreement with so many about it, you have this static reality that is this wonderful platform that you stand on so solidly. And we want you to understand that this *reality* that you think is so stable and solid is not at all static—it's changing constantly. It's changing and becoming and morphing to the degree that you, in your physicalness, will *allow* it to be.

We want you to catch a glimpse of the way your physical world looks through the eyes of Source. Because when you begin to see your world through the eyes of Source, then you begin to distract yourself, to turn the other cheek, to withdraw your attention from the aspects of your planet and life on this planet that you do not want to replicate and repeat and teach to your children . . . and, instead, you turn your attention to the aspects that you *do* want to hold into your vibration, that you *do* want the *Law of Attraction* to respond to.

Now, you don't need to worry about the *Law of Attraction*'s response. It is always turned on. *The Law of Attraction switch—always on.* Which means, *whatever it is that you are offering vibrationally is being responded to.* But the thing that most of you do not realize is that there are two aspects of your Being to which the *Law of Attraction* is responding: *There is the Non-Physical part of you,* which, we've been explaining to you, is always Non-Physically focused (and can you imagine how long that's been going on?). *Then there's the physical you that's been going on as long as the physical you has been going on, which is not that long.*

So, there is *this* part of you that the *Law of Attraction* is responding to and *this* part of you that the *Law of Attraction* is responding to. And what we want you to realize is the larger part of you is the dominant part of you, because the *Law of Attraction* is responding not only to who you were before you were born, but (hear this) to *who-you-really-are* as a result of being here in this physical body. Can you get it that this life experience is causing the greater part of you to expand and become? Do you know that that's why you came to begin with?

Humans tell a story that is so irrational that goes something like: "So Source is perfect, and I've been sent here to figure out how to get perfect. And Source has laid down *Laws* for me to learn, and I'll learn them, and I'll persevere, and I'll reach for the perfection that Source has achieved." And we want you to understand that *that Source that you are talking about is always within you. You cannot get yourself away from it. You can pinch yourself off pretty good, but the*

Source that is within you is always within you; and you can tell by the way you feel to what degree your thoughts, in the moment, are allowing the fullness of Source—or not.

When you feel *love* for yourself or for another, you are a perfect Vibrational Match to the Source within you. When you feel *hatred* or *anger* toward someone else or toward yourself, you are nowhere near the vibrational equivalent of your Source—and the vibrational variance between who you're letting yourself be and *who-you-really-are* is noted to you by your negative emotion. *Negative emotion,* whatever degree of it you're experiencing, always means to that degree you're pinching yourself off from the fullness of *who-you-are.*

When you allow yourself, in your physical human form, to ride the rocket of desire that the Source within you is riding, you feel *passion,* you feel *enthusiasm,* you feel *love,* you feel *certainty,* you feel *flexibility* and *vitality,* you are *energized . . . you are in love with life—* that is *who-you-really-are.* And when you feel *frustration,* when you feel *overwhelment,* when you feel *anger* or *greater anger,* when you feel *rage* or *disappointment,* when you feel *fear* or *depression,* you are pinching yourself off incrementally more and more and more and more from *who-you-really-are.*

And so, we want you to understand that the emotions that you feel are (in every moment that you are feeling them, whether they feel like *love* or whether they feel like *despair)—the emotion that you are feeling is always, every single time, your indicator of your vibrational relationship between who life has caused you to become and who you're letting yourself be, right here in this moment, by virtue of whatever it is you're giving your attention to.*

Talk about moment-by-moment, segment-by-segment Guidance! Talk about always having a bead on *who-you-really-are* and what you really want and where you said you really want to go. In other words, this is sophisticated *Guidance* that is with you always once you learn to read it.

Your navigational systems in your vehicles are similar. They know where you are, and you program in your desired destination and the system calculates the route between where you are and where you want to be—and your *Guidance System* is the same way.

Here you stand, maybe with not enough money or with a relationship that feels awful or with a bodily condition that isn't pleasing you or is frightening you. Here you stand in that contrasting experience, sending out rockets of desires, constantly, for an improved experience—more rockets now than ever before, because knowing what you *don't* want helps you to identify what you *do* want. And the Source within you not only rides those rockets, but becomes the vibrational equivalent of the new-and-expanded you.

So, the question that we want to put to you is: *Are you, right now—by virtue of what you're thinking and speaking—are you letting yourself keep up with you? Are you keeping up with who life has caused you to become?* And if you are, then you're tuned in, tapped in, turned on—you feel great. If you are, then you are allowing yourself to be that extended version of you. *Then you are seeing the world through the eyes of Source.*

If you are feeling negative emotion, it means that something has your attention, and it is certainly valid. In other words, we know you don't make this stuff up; you are observing it. You're not deliberately trying to hold yourself apart from *who-you-are,* but anytime you feel negative emotion, you are nevertheless doing exactly that: You're holding yourself apart from *who-you-are.*

Living a Vibrational Match?

We want to show you how to recognize your own *Guidance System* and how to more effectively utilize it, moment by moment. We want you to leave this gathering with a newfound resolve that how you feel matters because how you feel is your indication of your alignment or misalignment with *who-you-are*—with your allowing of the whole of *who-you-are* to be present in this moment or of your resisting of *who-you-really-are* to be present in this moment.

Many physical Beings are moving around through life a mere shadow of *who-they-are.* Mothers are shouting angrily at their children when there is no one on the planet that they want to love more—out of control, not knowing how to hold themselves in the vibration of love because they're having knee-jerk responses to life.

And we want you to begin to utilize the contrast in a *deliberate, conscious, comprehensive* way.

We want you to understand the components of life. When you get *who-you-are,* and when you get how *who-you-really-are* feels, and when you start tuning yourself to that feeling, you will begin to be a Vibrational Match to *who-you-really-are.* And, when you're tuned in, tapped in, turned on—when you are offering the vibration that comes from the core of your Being—your power of influence is so huge that others who are watching you are amazed at the confidence and power with which you move through life. When you are a Vibrational Match to *who-you-are,* the *Law of Attraction* brings to you, surrounds you with, lines up for you a steady stream of powerful, joyful opportunities and openings that just leads you, segment by segment, toward an ever-evolving, always-unfolding, joyful life experience.

It's not about knowing what you *don't* want so you know what you *do* want and then you have to figure out how to get over there to what you *do* want. We're not talking about the handful—or dozen or hundreds or even thousands—of things that you are wanting. This workshop is not about getting you *to* those things. This workshop is about helping you to reorient your understanding of why you are here in this body to begin with.

You did not come forth to "get it done." You did not come forth to identify things you want and then move over to live the manifestation of them because the manifestation of them is better than the absence of them. You came forth in order to identify what you want so that you could move in the direction of what you want so that you can enjoy the Stream of Life that is constant and Eternal. You want to be in the flow of *who-you-are,* not bucking the Current.

The *Law of Attraction* and its response to this powerful you that you have become creates a Current that feels to you like a river or stream that is always moving in the direction of that which life has caused you to become. And when you let yourself go *with* that flow, you feel those emotions that you describe as positive emotions. But when you're turned *upstream* in *opposition* to that current, you feel it in your body; you feel it in every fiber of your being. You feel it because you are not letting yourself be *who-you-are*. And that contradiction in Energy tears you apart. It makes you miserable. It messes up your body. It ruins your life to some degree. It keeps you from being *who-you-are*.

Now, when you croak, of course that all ends. Because when you croak (we love that disrespectful word . . . since there is no death, we try to be as disrespectful of your idea of it as we can)—when you have what you call your death experience (your croaking experience)—you stop beating the drum of all of the things that you've been worrying about in your physical form, and the vibration of *who-you-are* becomes dominant.

In one fell swoop, you become the Being that all that you have lived has caused you to become. But we are wanting to submit to you that you do not have to croak to have that happen. You can stay right here in this physical body, and you can—moment to moment, day by day—by caring about how you *feel,* tune yourself to the vibration of the center of your Being. And as you tune yourself to *who-you-really-are*, then you will begin to understand how good life feels and how good life is supposed to feel for you. Life is supposed to feel good.

Jerry and Esther had a wonderful experience last summer: They went white-water river rafting. And as they took their raft down to the river's edge . . . (There were many of them: six of them that went together and many others—dozens, really, of high school wrestlers—in the other boats. It was a remarkable day of splashing one another. The high school wrestlers didn't start it; Jerry and Esther's friends did . . . but once it got started, it was a very wet day.) . . . as they got to the river's edge, none of them, not one of them, even considered turning the boat *upstream* and paddling *against* the current. It was so perfectly obvious that that very fast-moving river was going to have its way with them.

And the river guide, almost the first thing he said to them was, "Friends, this is not Disneyland, and we cannot turn this river off." He was wanting them to understand the power of this river. And we want to say exactly the same thing to you: We want you to understand the power of this river and the fact that we cannot turn this river off. You set your river in motion long before you came forth into this physical body. And this river has been moving very fast since you've been in this physical body. And every time you know what you *don't want,* you make the river go a little faster by offering the rocket of desire about what you're *wanting.*

The reason the river moves faster and faster and faster is because every time you identify, at any level of your Being, a preference or a desire of how life would be better for you, the Non-Physical part of you embraces that thought so completely and holds it so unequivocally and becomes the vibrational offerer of it so completely. And then, as the powerful *Law of Attraction* responds to that ever-increasing amassing vibration that you are setting forth, there is a powerful sucking feeling that is drawing you toward it. (Are you getting a sense of this?)

We're trying to get you to understand how fast this river is moving and how important it is that you let yourself go with it. When you let yourself move in the direction of who you've become, you feel the ease of going with that flow. And when you turn in opposition to it, you feel the dis-ease of not allowing yourself to go with the flow. And every emotion you feel is about simply that.

If you feel negative emotion, what it means, every single time, is: Life has caused you to become something more than this thought, this action, this word is allowing you to be. In other words, "Life helps me to know that I want more money—and the Source Energy part of me becomes a more prosperous Being."

Can you imagine (we *know*) how much abundance is amassed for you in your Vibrational Escrow. There are veritable fortunes there calling you to them. So, here's all of this abundance that you, in all your lives, have set forth there. And here you are, often saying, "I don't have enough money"—more important, feeling the disappointment of not having enough money.

"I don't have enough money. I don't have enough money. I would like to buy that, but I can't afford it. I wish I could buy that, but I can't afford it. I'm so tired of wanting things that I cannot have. I'm so tired of not having enough money. I don't have enough money. I don't have enough money. I don't have enough money. I don't have enough money. I don't have enough money. I don't have enough money. Hardly anybody I know has enough money. [Fun] Hardly anybody I know has enough money. I don't know anybody who has enough money. Nobody has enough money. Nobody has enough money. Nobody has enough money. That rich bugger over there's got plenty of money. [Fun] That rich bugger over there's got plenty of money—much, much more than his fair share of money. He squanders it and wastes it on unnecessary things. Don't you know there are people starving? [Fun] I don't have enough money. I don't have enough money. I don't have enough money. He probably deals drugs. [Fun] I don't have enough money. I don't have enough money. I don't have enough money. I don't have enough money. I don't have enough money."

And we want you to understand that you can't *feel* that way and let your money in. You just can't. The vibrational frequencies are too far apart.

Your disappointment is your indicator that you're not letting money in—and no money coming in is an indicator, too. In other words, there are emotional indicators of how you're doing, and then there's post-manifestational awareness, yes? We want you to realize that whatever you're living is the indicator of what you're doing, vibrationally. But even more . . . (Oh, we so want you to hear this. We're going to stay here till you get this. [Fun] It'll only take a minute.) . . . *what you're living is the indicator of what you're offering vibrationally.* Now, how does that sentence sound to you? Does it sound important? *What you're living is the indicator of your vibration* sounds important, but we don't want it to be so important, for this reason: *It's only an <u>indicator</u> of a vibration.*

"My bank account is an indicator of vibration. I hate what's in my bank account. There's so little in my bank account. Why doesn't my bank account get bigger? Why doesn't it get bigger? Why doesn't it get bigger? Why doesn't it get bigger? Why doesn't it get bigger? Why doesn't it get bigger? Why doesn't it get bigger? Why doesn't it get bigger?" Because it's an indicator of *why* it doesn't get bigger, *why* it doesn't get bigger. . . .

"My body is hurting me. It feels so uncomfortable. And I so want my body to begin feeling better. I've been given these diagnoses, and I don't like what's happening to my body." *Your body and what you're living is an indicator of your vibration.* Period. "I don't know what's happening to my body. I can't control my body. I don't know what's happening. I'm afraid. I don't know what to do. . . ." Everything that you are living is nothing more than an indicator of the drum that you're beating—that's all.

People talk about the reality of their life as if it is important. And we want you to understand, it's only the temporary indicator. Do you go to the gas station—your gas gauge is on empty—do you go to the gas station and look at your gas gauge in horror? "How did this happen? [Fun] Why, why, why did this happen to me?" Do you lay your head on the steering wheel and just sob? "Oh, look what it's come to. [Fun] I'm finished. I've lived all of this life, and look where I am." Or do you just fill up?

And yet, you'll have something happening with your body, and you walk so slowly into the doctor's office with fear gripping your heart because he might tell you the very thing that you don't want to know. He might take his tools and look deep into the recesses of your body, in places that you cannot see, and he might tell you that there is an *indicator* in your body. And we want you to say, "Good to know. Nice to know. Didn't need you to tell me; I know. I can feel the discord."

Whatever you're living, whether it is about your body or whether it is about your relationship or whether it is about your money—no matter what it is about—whatever you're living is only a temporary, in-the-moment indicator of your temporary, in-the-moment vibrational offering. That's all it is.

The only problem is, you don't know that your vibrational offering is *temporary* because you've been speaking those words for so long, they're stuck in your vibrational craw. You've been telling the same story for so long, you don't know any new stories. Somehow, you got convinced that you should "tell it like it is."

Now, let's play that over what we were just saying: "Tell it like it is." Your mother says, "Tell me the *truth* of *what-is*." So you say, "I don't have enough money. I don't have enough money . . . I hate you. I hate you. I hate you. I hate you . . . I don't like what you're doing. I don't like what you're doing with my money. I don't like what you're doing with my government. I don't like what you're doing. . . ." We're making a point here, and we know it's getting annoying to you. [Fun] But we want you to understand that *you've got to tell a different story.*

Did we make a point with you about these two points of vibrational offerings that are going on—there's the *larger you,* and then there's the *physical you?* Do you get that? Do you believe it? Do you understand that you are this Source Energy Being? So, listen to the difference in the drums that are being beat: "I don't have enough money. I don't have enough money. I don't have enough money. I don't have enough money. I've never had enough money. . . . There's plenty of money. The money is here. The things are lined up. The resources are in place. Circumstances and events have been arranged. The money is here. The money is here. Look over here. Look over here. Look over here. Look over here."

Now, we want to depict the emotional difference: "I don't have enough money. I don't have enough money. Why don't I have enough money? I'm so sorry that I don't have enough money. What have I done wrong? I should have known better. *They* should have known better."

There's plenty of money. Nothing has gone wrong. Everything that you want is lined up for you. Whenever you're ready, it's right here for you. There's nothing you need to do; you've done all the work. All you need to do is relax and allow what you want to flow into your experience. You want to begin to listen to the drum of the Source within you. You want to listen to the call of Source. Source is calling you in the direction of what you want. And the way that you know that you're moving in the direction is because things start lightening up for you, meaning that they begin feeling really, really good to you.

When you get on this track of following the trail that has been prepaved by you and is being tended by the Source within you and is calling you toward what you are wanting—you feel energized. You feel enthusiasm. And yet, you know what your physical world trains you to do? Your physical world says, "If it feels good, you need to be wary."

You say to your friends, "Oh, I'm so excited about this." And they say, "Watch out. Watch out—that positive emotion could mean something's going very, very wrong for you. [Fun] I've known other people who were positive and bad things happened to them. I think you'd better play it safe. I think you'd better stay right where you are. I know he beats you, but he makes a good living. . . ."

And what we're wanting you to understand is: *The way you feel is everything, because the way you feel is your indication of whether you're closing the gap between who you're letting yourself be and who-you-really-are—or whether you're widening the gap.*

You're going to get so that you can feel statement by statement whether it's *downstream* or *upstream, downstream* or *upstream.* The *downstream* statement always feels like *relief.* It doesn't always feel like sunshine, lollipop, and roses—it doesn't always feel like the best feeling thing that you've ever felt—but the *downstream* thought from where you stand always feels better than the *upstream* thought. You can always tell the difference between something that feels a little worse and a little better, a little worse and a little better.

Often, a gathering like this leaves you with the impression that you need to get over here into these good-feeling emotions. And you have been so sick to your stomach of positive people for so long that the idea of being one of them is abhorrent to most of you. In other words, nothing is so annoying as to see someone happy when you're not. Nothing is more annoying than to see someone living the life you want to live when you're not living it, and, even worse, crowing about it: "Oh, let me tell you how good my life is." "Let's not go there," you say. [Fun]

We don't want you to compare yourself with anybody else. We just want you to have a comparative awareness of whether this thought that you're thinking right now is upstream or downstream. And do you know why? Because this thought that you are thinking right now is your point of attraction. This is the thought that you're thinking right now that your life is becoming the indicator of. But there's this one little thing that we need to tell you (you probably already know it): *There's a buffer of time between you offering a vibration and it manifesting. More than 99 percent of every creation is completed by you vibrationally before the evidence begins to show.* So, you can be turned in the *downstream* direction for a while before you begin to see the evidence of it. And that's what makes you not know. You want instant manifestation.

Can you imagine Jerry and Esther on the river with their guide, telling him, "Oh, we like instant manifestation. So we don't want to take all the time to ride down the river. Put our boat back on the bus. Let's *drive* down the canyon. It will be a lot faster. Put it in a few hundred yards from where we're going to take it out, and we'll just be done with this." And he would say, "I thought you wanted a ride on the river." [Fun]

And that's what we want you to understand: *You want this ride on the river. You want to discern contrast.* Oh, you think that if you had the choice (and you did)—but you think that if you'd had the choice *from this physical experience* (and good thing you didn't)— you think that if you had the choice (and you did) that if you came forth into this physical experience, that your nest would be so feathered that it would be full of all of the things that you want, and there would be nothing in your environment that would even get your attention a little bit that would make you feel bad.

Many of you as parents try to do that for your children, and you deprive them temporarily of the contrast that they came to live. You said, "I'll go forth into the contrast, and from it I will be able to discern what I prefer. And that would be a wonderful thing, because when I know what I prefer, I'll hold it in my vibrational countenance, and then the *Law of Attraction* will bring it to me. And then I'll have a new platform from which to prefer. And I'll hold it in my vibrational countenance, and *Law of Attraction* will bring it to me. So, from this buffet of life, I will extract from it the things that I most prefer, and out of it, I will carve out the perfect life for me, from my personal perspective."

But, instead, you got here, and there were so many other "dysfunctional" people around you who had already lost sight of their own *Guidance System,* who said to most of you: "I am a very conditional lover and liver of life—which means good conditions make me feel good, but bad conditions make me feel bad. So, these are the rules for the good conditions that I need to extract from you. And since you're in my life, I'll be looking at you quite a lot. (Since I am your employer, or since I am your mother, or since I am your father, or since I am your teacher, I have been assigned the task of looking at you.) And when I look at you, I want to feel good, which means you need to perform in ways that make *me, me, me, me, me* feel good. I don't want *you* to be selfish. You need to behave in ways that make *me* (I'm your selfless mother) feel good. [Fun] And if I see any of those things that make me feel bad, you will be in such trouble."

Which would be all right if there could only have been one of them and they were always in agreement with themselves. But they are so fickle, and there are so many of them and they want different things from you—and you just can't stand on your head in enough different ways to make them happy. And, pretty soon, you figure out that no matter how hard you try, you can't make them happy. *We are wanting to say to you that none of you came forth with the intention of listening to anyone outside of you. Every one of you knew that life would cause you to expand, and that that expanded Being would call you, and when you go in the direction of that expansion, that you would feel good. And you planned on leaving everybody else out of the equation. (You really did.)*

You did not plan on guiding your life by that which other people are saying. First of all, they don't have very much of an attention span. (Have you noticed?) How long did your lover really give you his undivided attention? No one dares say. *Not that long. Not that long.* [Fun] How long did your mother give you her undivided attention? *Not very long.* Nobody can do it because nobody is born to be the keeper of you. They are all born to be the creator of their own experience. And . . . we think that the greatest hypocrisy (the thing that has caused you the most trouble) is that they tell you that you are important to them, but the bottom line is, how they *feel* is what's most important to them. So, they keep trying to guide you and your behavior by what makes *them* feel good.

And then, oh, you get so full of resentment because you know what would make your life really wonderful right away is if you could just accept that everybody is in this life for themselves. *And that's not a bad thing, because what that's really saying is, everybody is Source Energy, and everybody came forth in order to give birth to new rockets of desire. And everyone has a Source within them that is guiding them toward their best interest. So, imagine what a wonderful world that is.*

If everyone has their own personal *Guidance System*, and it is *Source*, and everyone is being called toward the improved life experience, and everyone—or even most of them, or even some of them—are hearing the call and moving toward it . . . can you imagine how magnificent this world would become?

Do you know that no one offers any violent, or what you would call *negative,* behavior who's in alignment with *Source?* It just does not happen. One hundred percent of what you call negative behavior happens because someone's out there on the raw-and-ragged edge—they're trying to fill the void; they're trying to get to someplace that they want to be—*but they're going about it in a way that cannot ever be.*

What Does Your Story Indicate?

So, we think we've made a very powerful point with you. We have given it everything Esther has. [Fun] We have projected to her the block of thought that says to you: *You are the creator of your experience, and you must create your experience* <u>deliberately</u> *if you are to have the joyful experience that you meant to have. Unless you, in any moment, are seeing the world through the eyes of Source, then you are but a shadow of the Being that you've come forth to be. Which means, if you are doing less than loving whatever it is you're giving your attention to, you are not who you were really born to be. Negative emotion means you've pinched yourself off, to some degree, from* <u>who-you-really-are.</u>

So, we talk about all of these powerful and wonderful positive emotions, but we would like you to just reach for one emotion, and let's just give it one simple label: *It is the emotion of* <u>relief.</u> And we want to say to you that no matter where you are—and here's something really important to acknowledge—*you are where you are.* "I am where I am. I am where I am, regarding my relationship, regarding my body, regarding my money, regarding my philosophies, regarding my worldview, regarding my family experiences—I am where I am relative to all things. And all that means is, I've practiced vibrations that have brought me to a point of consistent attraction on every subject imaginable."

In other words, nothing that you're living is just happening to you. It's all happening in response to the thoughts, and the patterns of thoughts, that you are offering. And most of it is pretty darn good, isn't it? In other words, we're just talking about some fine-tuning here. We're just talking about some deliberate leaning in the direction more of what you're wanting.

The reason that we are so enthusiastic about presenting this to you in this way is because we know that if you leave this gathering understanding that *you* are the point of attraction for you, and that you are offering a vibrational signal that the *Law of Attraction* is replicating, and that you can tell by the way you feel how well you're keeping up with what life has caused you to become, or not—and once the only thing that is important to you is that you feel good; once you begin guiding your thought, word, and behavior because of the way it *feels,* rather than because of the *truth* of it; once you begin to care more about how you feel than anything else—you will then be the joyous, Deliberate Creator that you came forth to be. And anything less than that leaves you pinched off from *who-you-really-are.*

So, the feeling of relief is what you're reaching for. And as we're moving through this day, we'll show you how to find thoughts that give you that feeling of relief.

We know that in any gathering, there is the tendency to want to speculate on endless things. And we're willing to talk with you about anything that is important to you. We just want you to remember that you are offering a vibrational signal now . . . that as you offer it for a little bit of time (it really doesn't take very long), it begins to set up a frequency that begins, then, the pattern of attraction. And so, it's really helpful if you begin right now to tell the story of your life the way you want it to be rather than the way that it has been. Because telling it the way it has been only holds you in that holding pattern of attraction.

Can you feel that anything that you would call *negative attraction* is really just the disallowance of the *positive attraction* that is already in motion? This is the thing that we want to ferret out in a way that you really hear it. There is not a source of darkness. You don't walk into a room and look for a dark switch. "Oh yeah, flip that and it lets that inky, misty stuff come into the room and cover up the light." You know that's not what's happening. There's not a source of badness or a source of evil or a source of sickness—there is only a disallowing of the Stream. There's only a disallowing of moving in the direction of that which life has caused you to become. That's all.

So, everything is so much simpler than you have thought, because this moment, where all of your power is, is the only moment in which you can activate a vibration. Oh, you can activate a vibration about something that happened a long time ago—but you're doing it *now.* You can remember something that happened a long time ago, or yesterday—but you're doing it *now.* You can anticipate something that will happen tomorrow, or ten years from now—but you're doing it *now.*

So, whatever you think causes you to offer a signal *now,* which is your point of attraction. And when you offer a point of attraction for as little as 17 seconds, the *Law of Attraction* kicks in. In other words, that's the combustion point where another thought that matches it joins it. Hold that thought for another 17 seconds and there's another combustion. Do that until you have achieved a vibrational alignment with any thought for as little as 68 seconds, and things begin to move enough that a discerning eye can see the manifestation has begun. That's all: *68 seconds of telling it the way you want it to be rather than telling it like it is. Are there things in your life that are as you want them to be? Keep telling that story. Are there things in your life that are not as you want them to be? Don't tell that story.*

"But I am really busy. I do have more to do than I can do. Did you hear what she said?" The good news is, you will never again beat a negative drum and not have conscious awareness of it. And that is such a good thing, because you cannot choose something that feels better until you are aware of what you are choosing. So, *relief* is the order of business.

What do you want to talk about?

The Vibrational Essence of Money?

Question: Thank you very much. This veritable fortune I've been amassing for so long, I was . . .

Abraham: Don't use sarcasm now. [Fun]

Question: I'd love a little bit more of your experience on how I can deliberately be leaning more towards *allowing* it.

Abraham: Now, anyone who listens back (and especially those who are sitting here in the room) might feel yourself wanting to say, especially by the end of the day, "Abraham is really nitpicking here." But we want you to feel, if you can, the *feeling-place* from which that question comes—in other words, this "veritable fortune," and we sensed a sort of mocking tone. "If there is . . . [Fun] where's my stuff? If the *Law of Attraction* is as you say, and I've been amassing this fortune, then where is it, and how can I get to it?"

And we want you to just feel, for a moment, what is the dominant vibration within that sentiment that you offered. Were you offering the vibration from the *lack* of the money or from the *having* of the money? [Lack]

And we know, you say, "Well, of course he is, because it isn't there yet. So, how can he offer a vibration about a state of being that he has not yet achieved?" And we say, you've just got to figure out how to do it, because until you do, you can't have the state of being that you want to achieve. *You have to find the vibrational essence of it.*

And we think it's logical that, in the beginning, there would be some questioning. "Where is it? What am I doing wrong? What should I do differently?" is really what you are saying. But we want you to feel the entrapment that your own words and attitude about things have. And so, the work is, *you have to find a way of distracting yourself from the absence of the money, while you activate within yourself a feeling of the money.*

So, things like *feeling appreciation for the prosperity that you are living, feeling appreciation for the possibility of more coming.* In fact, we'd like to say that even when you get into an *attitude of hope,* you're much closer in vibration to allowing it than when you are in the *vibration of doubt.*

So, we teased you about a little bit of sarcasm about this "veritable fortune," but we want you to realize that *when you feel sarcastic,* *when you feel _pessimistic,_ it's a far cry from feeling _optimistic_ and _hopeful._* So, the answer to your question, "How do I let my fortune come to me, and me come to my fortune?"—it's by pretending that it's already done. By taking pieces of the fortune and mentally spending it. By imagining how much fun it will be to have it. By enjoying the feeling of relief, even before you have the actual reason to feel the relief. By caring so much about the way you feel that you guide your thoughts apart from the reality.

And so, *sarcasm* (we're really kidding you a tiny little bit about that) is further from letting it in than *optimism* or *positive expectation*. So, feel the difference between saying, "My money is really slow in coming. I'm starting to believe that it's in Vibrational Escrow for me, but I can't figure out how to let it in." Feel that sentiment. And then feel the difference between that and saying, "It's going to be nice when I figure this out. It's going to be nice when I figure this out"—let the resistance go. "I haven't figured it out— I've been working at this a long time, and I haven't figured it out" is totally *upstream* and resistant in nature. "I'm looking forward to figuring this out" releases resistance.

"It'll be nice when I figure this out. I have glimpses of this in my experience every day. I get it on a lot of different subjects. I'm doing pretty good on much of this. I do like knowing that there is a fortune that's been amassed for me. I do like knowing that my life experience has caused me to put some things in Vibrational Escrow. I do like realizing that the Source within me has preceded me in its expectation of my receiving of that.

"I do like knowing that my negative emotion itself is my indicator that I've departed from how Source sees me. I do like knowing that negative emotion is my indicator that Source sees me as prosperous, and in the moment of my negative emotion, I'm not. I do like the idea that Source can guide me to more positive feelings, and I do like knowing that the negative feelings are my indicator that I'm not going in the direction that Source is thinking. I do like knowing that.

"I'm pretty good at this; I am aware of the way I feel—I can tell the difference. I have noticed the correlation between what I've been thinking and feeling and what's manifesting. I do know that the reality shifts to match my chronic feeling. And I do understand that thinking something in the beginning that is different from what I've been thinking takes a little bit more focus. I do know that when I focus a little longer, it gets easier and easier. And I do know that the *longer* I say something, then the *easier* it is to say it, and the *more* I say it, the *easier* it is for me to *expect* it. And I do know that *expectation* brings a different feeling. I do know the difference in the feeling of *hope* and the feeling of *doubt*. I do know the difference in the feeling of *excitement* and the feeling of *discouragement*. I can do this. I know I can do this." Just conversations like that make all the difference in the world. That is the work.

We know it feels slow going, but that's the work. You didn't come to your chronic thought all at once. (And by *chronic,* we don't mean negative necessarily. By chronic we mean, *what I usually think about this subject*.) You came to it gradually. And you're not going to shift from it all at once. You're going to shift from it gradually. . . . If you want to shift from it all at once, you're not going to do it—and then you'll get *discouraged*. But if you expect to shift from it gradually, and you do it, then you feel *encouraged*—so, just one statement at a time, telling the story the way you like it, the way you want it to be.

So, this is the way we would tell your story: "I have recently heard that there is a *veritable fortune* waiting for me in Vibrational Escrow. And I like how that sounds. And the idea of my life experience and what I'm living being the reason that it's there is really thrilling to me. I like the idea that I can be or do or have whatever I want. And so, I'm beginning to tell my story the way I want it to be. I don't think that money is the path to happiness, but I don't think it's the root of all evil either. I think money is a route to freedom. I think that within more money there are more choices, and in more choices—there is more fun. I like the idea of making decisions about what I want to do based on how it feels to do it rather than on whether I can afford to do it or not.

"I like the opportunities that more money opens for me, and so I don't think I'm just excited about the veritable fortune that's waiting for me. I think I'm excited about what that means to me and my family, what that means to those around me, what that means to the way I begin to view life, what that means to the way I experience life. It's exciting to me to think about those kinds of changes.

"I love my life in so many ways, but I can see how this money that's on its way to me will enhance my life in *this* way and *this* way and *this* way. An extra hundred dollars today would mean *these* changes. An extra thousand dollars today would mean *these* changes. If I were allowing in an extra hundred thousand dollars this year, I would do *this* with it. If I allowed in an extra five hundred thousand dollars every year, oh, that would mean I would live over *there*. And that means I would drive *that*. And that means I would work . . . that means I *wouldn't* work there." [Fun] Just play with it in your mind—envision.

We've offered a lot of games, and the most productive game that we've ever seen (and we've watched a lot of people apply these processes)—and this is a powerful, powerful game—is: *Put $100 in your pocket with the intention of <u>mentally</u> spending it every day, over and over and over and over again. Just contemplate how many things, if you wanted to, you could exchange for that $100.*

It is amazing what that simple game does in shifting the way you feel about money. It frees you up, because your habit is to say, "Oh, I want that but I shouldn't"—where this $100 says, "I could if I wanted to. I could if I wanted to. *I can do that.*" So, instead of saying, "I can't afford that," over and over and over again, you're saying, "I could if I wanted to. I could if I wanted to. I could if I wanted to. I could if I wanted to."

Someone said, "Well, Abraham, you haven't been physical lately, because $100 doesn't buy much." And we said, *if you spend $100 a thousand times today, you've spent the equivalent of $100,000 today—and that goes a long way in shifting your vibration.* And then, people often say, "But it's not real." And we say, it *will be. It will be. You've got to <u>feel</u> it first, and once the vibration is stable within you—the realization of it has to come.*

The *Law of Attraction* must bring you the path, the method, the co-creators, and the results that you are conjuring vibrationally. *When you conjure prosperity in your vibration, prosperity must come in real life experience, and it will come in so many ways—it will come as you turn every corner. Everywhere you look, another huge evidence of prosperity will show itself to you once you get it just a little more active than what you've already got active.*

It's not the big deal you all make it out to be. You know why it feels like a big deal? Because you've been looking at *what-is,* offering a vibration of *what-is,* getting more of *what-is* for so long, you say, "I've done all this *effort,* and I've offered all this *work,* and I've *worked* all these years—and, in all of that, I've only come to where I am now. And so, what will that scanty little effort provide me when I've offered all this effort and I've only got this far?" And we say, you've been offering *action effort,* and now we're encouraging you to offer *vibrational effort. Vibrational effort is bringing you into usage of the power and Energy that creates worlds.*

Vibrational change makes big manifestational change when you are consistent in it, but when you say, "I want it but, I want it but, I want it but, I want it but," you don't make any headway. When you say, "I want it because, I want it because, I want it because, I want it because, I want it because," you make headway.

When you say, "I believe I can do it. I think I can do it. I doubt I can do it. I'm not really doing it. I believe I can do it. I would like to do it, but I doubt I can do it. I am not really doing it. But I'd like to do it. I'd really like to do it, but I can't do it because I haven't been doing it. But I'd like to do it. I really want to do it, but I'm not doing it. Hardly anybody does it. But I'd like to do it, but I want to do it, but it's hard to do it, and I'm not making any headway. And I want to do it, but I don't know what to do . . ." then nothing changes. It's the same old, same old, mundane, chronic vibrational habit of "the way I feel." *You have to use your willpower to focus your thoughts into a different story line. So, tell us now the story of your financial picture.*

My Story of Financial Success

Question: *All is well*—that's what I can think through that whole conversation, that all is well. And I feel that inside. It feels so wonderful and so organic, in a way. And I guess that's just my question: Is that part of the process?

Abraham: *That's all of the process,* because as we said, 99 percent of all creation is completed vibrationally before you get the evidence of it. So it's like traveling from Phoenix to San Diego, and San Diego's where you *want* to be, but for most of the distance of 400 miles, you're *not* where you want to be. And if it frustrates you that you're not there, vibrationally speaking you would just turn around and go back to Phoenix. You would never get there. But in terms of this physical journey from place to place, you say, "Well, I understand *that* journey, so I can make *that.* I can see my progress. I can see that with every mile I stay focused in that direction, that I'm getting farther from where I *don't* want to be and closer to where I *do* want to be."

And we say, so you keep the faith because you have this evidence that shows you you're getting close, you're getting closer, you're getting closer. So (unless you're walking) nobody gets discouraged about that journey. In other words, you hold the faith. You hold the belief. You don't say, "San Diego is an impossible dream." You don't say, "San Diego's *incurable*—I've tried and tried and tried and tried, and I can't get there," because you *can* get there, and you know you can.

When you make the connection that *the way you feel is your indicator of the direction that you're moving,* and you can honestly say to yourself, "I do *feel* optimistic—when I say, 'All is well,' I mean it . . . I really *feel* it," then we say, then you can't *not* get there. If you can maintain that expectation and that attitude and that vibrational frequency, it has to come—and it will come fast.

So you say, "Okay, I'm on my way. I've talked to Abraham, and Abraham went on for way more than 68 seconds, and I got the feeling of the vibration of it. And when I said, *'All is well,'* I really felt it. And then I looked at my real-life situation, and I saw I wasn't yet in 'San Diego.' In other words, I looked at something, and I felt the negative hit of it because I'm not where I want to be (I want to do something, and I don't have the money to do it), and I felt the disappointment."

And we say, good. The *disappointment* is your *indicator* that whatever just happened caused you to lose your sense of *expectation* and to begin focusing upon something different from your expectation. What can you do now to bring yourself back to that feeling?

When you work in that feeling of discouragement to bring yourself to something that feels better, you clean up your vibration in a way that it will never return to that negative place again. In other words, when you feel negative emotion and you take the time to chew on it (as we are here) until you actually feel relief—which will take you, usually, 68 seconds or more to get there—*when you actually, viscerally, feel the relief, now you're never going to have to clean up that vibration again on that subject in just that way. You moved in the Universe. You moved to a different vibrational vantage point.*

And here's the most important thing that we want you to hear about that: *Because you moved to a different vibrational vantage point, the manifestational evidence has to shift, too. So, in the moment that you make the effort to do that, all things in the Universe regarding that subject respond to the new vibration that you're offering.*

So, that's the day you get an idea that pays off for you. That's the day you rendezvous with somebody who has something to offer you—and you have something to offer them—and you exchange something, financially, as a result of it. In other words, that little bit of effort—you couldn't see that it was getting you closer to "San Diego"; you couldn't see it because it's not like driving your car toward a destination, but you felt it, so you knew it; and because you *felt* it, and because you understood the importance of the way you felt, you kept it up, and you kept it up, and you kept it up, and you kept it up . . . and pretty soon you don't just *hope* that you'll have your abundance—you don't just *believe* it—you *know* it, because the evidence is so emphatically surrounding you.

Just thought by thought by thought by thought by thought by thought, you clean it up, clean it up, clean it up, clean it up. What do we mean by "clean it up"? *You tell it the way you <u>want</u> it to be, and tell it less the way you <u>don't want</u> it to be. You stop <u>facing</u> reality, and you start <u>creating</u> reality.*

So your friends say, "What are you up to?"

And you say, "All good things."

And they say, "Were you able to buy that thing you wanted to buy? Or did you get that job you wanted to get?"

And you say, "I'm right on track with it."

And they say, "No, you didn't understand my question. [Fun] Did you *get* it?"

And you say, "You didn't understand my answer. I'm on track for it."

And they say, "Well, if you don't have it, you don't have it."

And you say, "Ah, not true at all. I have it *vibrationally*. And now that I've got it vibrationally, it must come to me—it is *Law. I've got it vibrationally.*"

"Well, how do you know it's coming?"

"Because I *feel* so good."

"Well, you feel good *before* you got it [Fun]—what's wrong with you?"

"I know the process. I have achieved vibrational alignment with my desire, and so it must come—it is *Law*."

"How do you know you've achieved vibrational alignment?" your negative friend says. "How do you know you've achieved vibrational alignment with what you want?"

"I feel good every time I think about it. I feel good when I think about my fortune. I don't feel sarcastic, and I don't feel disappointed, and I don't feel discouraged. I feel optimistic because I know it's coming. In fact, I'm so optimistic, look at my list of what I'm going to *do* with it. This is my list of what I'm going to do with it."

There's another game that we offer. It's a checkbook game where you deposit $1,000 into your account (vibrational dollars), and you spend that $1,000. On the second day, you deposit $2,000 and spend them. On the third day, you deposit $3,000 and spend them. . . . On the 365th day, you deposit $365,000 and spend it.

So, as you are spending this money (vibrationally)—as you are *mentally* spending it—what's happening is, you are creating outlets out there for it to go. . . . When you create a vibrational outlet, it draws everything for the accomplishment of it through you. That's what *eagerness* is. That's what *passion* is. That's what your feeling of *enthusiasm* is.

In other words, when you present, in this time-space reality, the vibrational prepaving of a desire, it sets things into motion that when you let yourself go with them—you feel wonderful. And when you don't let yourself go with them—you feel awful. (Did you hear that?) That means that if you feel really bad about something, it means you have asked for something, and the larger part of you has become something that you're not letting the rest of you keep up with.

We want you to realize that you're the reason that your Stream moves as fast as it does, and you are also the reason that you are pointed with or against the Current—and everything you *feel* is about that.

Everything that you want is because you think you will feel better in the having of it. Whether it's money or a material object or a relationship or an experience, circumstance, event—*everything that you want is because you think if you had it, you would feel better; and when you discover that just the <u>idea</u> of it will make you feel better, now you've achieved the <u>vibrational essence</u> of it. And then, the <u>Law of Attraction</u> has to yield it to you in all of the intricate details that your life has caused you to carve out for yourself. It has to be; and, in fact, it <u>is.</u>*

In your environment today, you are projecting (because of what you're living now) into the future improved life experience, that when new Energies are born into new infant bodies who are not resistant, they will then (because they're new and not resistant) reap the benefit of what you have put into the Mass Consciousness's Vibrational Escrow—just as you, in *your* time and space, are reaping the benefits of what past generations have set forward—because you just can't live life as humanity without asking for improvement. What we are wanting to propose to you is that you don't have to croak to close your gap, and you don't have to be reborn in order to reap the benefit of what you have launched. You can do it all here and now in this lifetime; and, in fact, that's what you planned.

You said, "I'll go forth, and the variety will inspire me to an idea. And once the idea has hatched within me, I will give it my undivided attention." Well, isn't that what we were just saying to you? *Give your undivided attention to your newly hatched desires, and never mind the reality that was the basis that caused you to want them.*

Let your awareness, instead of being: *"This is where I am"*—this is the thing that we most want this seminar to say to you in a way that you can hear it—be: *It doesn't matter where you are because it's so temporary.* It's just like the indicator on your gas gauge. Have you noticed how quickly it moves [Fun], especially lately? In other words, it's just an *indicator,* that's all it is. It's an *indicator.*

So, what's manifesting is just a temporary indicator of a temporary vibration. But you say, "Well, it didn't feel all that temporary because I've been living it for a long time." And we say, it's because you've been having the *same* responses and offering the *same* vibration, so it's the *same* thing happening—but it's *new. You're not living the same life. It's a new living of a new life from a new vibration. It's just that the vibration that you're offering now is the same one that you offered yesterday because you've got the habit of thinking of things the way you thought of them yesterday.*

If you've been away from the home that you grew up in for a while or away from the people that were there when you were growing up, and if the home and if the people are still there, go there soon and see how well you fit as you realize how much has happened in your life that has made you so different than who you were when you lived there. And then realize that in every moment of every day, this sort of expansion is taking place within you.

We love your question. We love the question: "How do I get from where I am to where I want to be?" And the answer is: *Look* in the direction of where you want to be, and *speak* in the direction of where you want to be, and never again look back over your shoulder about where you have come from. And if you can pull that one off, as soon as tomorrow you'll have evidence of your "veritable fortune."

Questioner: Astounding, thank you.

Boston Workshop Closing

Abraham: We have enjoyed this interaction. We've enjoyed every interaction with everyone who sat in the chair today. We've enjoyed the willingness of those of you who are sitting out there listening to it to patiently reach for the nugget that must be buried in there somewhere.

We tell you what we tell you not so that you can get to the results that you think you want, but so that you can feel the palpable relief and know that you can find it again anytime you reach for it.

We don't guide you toward manifestations because we think those manifestations are essential to your experience. We guide you toward successful creation of manifestations because we want you to get a handle on your own vibration—because your own vibration is your life, right now.

What you feel right now is a mixture of who you've become and who you're letting yourself be. And nothing other than that is ever true. And when you have conscious awareness of the tools in your bag of tricks that help you to turn in the direction of *who-you-are,* now you have the tools that help you to be the joyful Being that you've come forth to be.

We don't want you to be a successful holder of millions of dollars, although you will be. We want you to be the joyful Being that is enjoying the discovery of how to become that. We want the ride on the river to be as important to you in your physical form as it was to you when you decided to come forth.

We want you to know what you *don't* want so that you can know what you *do* want, and we want you to feel the difference. We want you to feel the relief when you turn in the direction of what you do want, and we want you to feel the knowing that you have improved your vibration, as you just did. And then we want you to feel the exhilaration of watching the Universal Forces converge around you and give you evidence of the alignment that took place. And then we want you to stand in that new platform, and we want you to feel the contrast that will launch yet another desire.

We want you to feel the power of the new desire and your vibrational relationship to it, and we want you to recognize that, once again, you're not up to speed with who life has caused you to become. But we want you to savor the knowledge that you now know what to do because you've done it so many times. And we want you to deliberately reach for the thought that feels better. *Reach for the thought that feels better, and move in the direction of what you are wanting—and then feel the new manifestation.*

We want you to get your hands in the clay of your life, and we want you to *like* molding the clay. We don't want it to be about getting to the result; we want it to be about the process of alignment. We want it to be about the Energy in your belly. We want it to be about the emotion that you can improve. We want it to be about you then recognizing the evidence that comes to you because you did improve the emotion.

We loved how you felt, and we loved how you *feel*. And we loved the fact that you couldn't feel how you feel if you hadn't felt how you felt. In other words, that vibrational relationship is life—and there's no wrong in any of it. It's all the molding of the clay.

We've enjoyed this more than words can say. Life is so good from our vantage point. We want you (we invite you) to look at your world through the eyes of us because what we see is really, really good! Good times are before you as a result of this gathering.

There is great love here for you. And, as always, we remain joyously incomplete.

Index

A

B

C

E

F

G

H

I

K

L

M

N

O

p

T

About the Authors

Excited about the clarity and practicality of the translated information from the Beings who called themselves *Abraham,* **Jerry** and **Esther Hicks** began disclosing their amazing Abraham experience to a handful of close business associates in 1986.

Recognizing the practical results being received by themselves and by those people who were asking meaningful questions regarding the application of the principles of the *Law of Atraction* to finances, bodily conditions, and relationships—and then successfully applying Abraham's answers to their own situations—Jerry and Esther made a deliberate decision to allow Abraham's teachings to become available to an ever-widening circle of seekers of answers to how to live a better life.

Using their San Antonio, Texas, conference center as their base, Esther and Jerry have traveled to approximately 50 cities a year since 1989, presenting a series of interactive *Law of Attraction* Workshops to those leaders who have gathered to participate in this progressive stream of thought. And although worldwide attention has been given to this philosophy of Well-Being by Leading Edge thinkers and teachers who have, in turn, incorporated many of Abraham's concepts into their best-selling books, scripts, lectures, films, and so forth, the primary spread of this material has been from person to person, as individuals begin to discover the value of this form of spiritual practicality in their personal life experiences.

Abraham—a group of obviously evolved Non-Physical teachers —speak their Broader Perspective through Esther. And as they speak to our level of comprehension through a series of loving, allowing, brilliant, yet comprehensively simple essays in print and in sound, they guide us to a clear Connection with our loving, guiding *Inner Being* and to uplifting self-empowerment from our Total Self.

Featuring the Universal *Law of Attraction,* the Hickses have now published more than 800 Abraham-Hicks books, cassettes, CDs, and DVDs. They may be contacted through their extensive interactive Website at: **www.abraham-hicks.com**; or by mail at Abraham-Hicks Publications, P.O. Box 690070, San Antonio, TX 78269.

Hay House Titles of Related Interest

YOU CAN HEAL YOUR LIFE, the movie, starring Louise L. Hay & Friends
(available as a 1-DVD program and an expanded 2-DVD set)
Watch the trailer at: **www.LouiseHayMovie.com**

-=‖ 🎬 ‖=-

THE LAWS OF THINKING: 20 Secrets to Using the Divine Power
of Your Mind to Manifest Prosperity, by Bishop E. Bernard Jordan

MAXIMIZE YOUR POTENTIAL THROUGH THE POWER OF YOUR
SUBCONSCIOUS MIND TO CREATE WEALTH AND SUCCESS,
by Dr. Joseph Murphy

QUANTUM SUCCESS: The Astonishing Science
of Wealth and Happiness, by Sandra Anne Taylor

THE RICHES WITHIN: Your Seven Secret Treasures,
by Dr. John F. Demartini

SECRETS OF SUCCESS: The Science and Spirit of Real Prosperity,
by Sandra Anne Taylor and Sharon A. Klingler

SUCCESS INTELLIGENCE: Essential Lessons and Practices
from the World's Leading Coaching Program on Authentic Success,
by Robert Holden, Ph.D.

21 DISTINCTIONS OF WEALTH: Attract the Abundance You Deserve,
by Peggy McColl

-=‖ 🎬 ‖=-

All of the above are available at your local bookstore,
or may be ordered by contacting Hay House (see next page).

-=‖ 🎬 ‖=-